DO YOUR
OWN MARKET
RESEARCH

Also available from Kogan Page:

The Market Research Series

Buying Market Research
Peter Jackson

Desk Research
Peter Jackson

Interviewing
Paul Hague

Presentations and Report Writing
Paul Hague and Kate Roberts

Questionnaire Design
Paul Hague

Sampling and Statistics
Paul Hague and Paul Harris

Other Market Research Books

The Effective Use of Market Research (Second Edition)
Robin Birn

Handbook of Market Research Techniques
Edited by Robin Birn, Paul Hague and Phyllis Vangelder

The Industrial Market Research Handbook (Third Edition)
Paul Hague

Marketing Research in Practice
Paul Hague and Peter Jackson

Researching Business Markets
Edited by Ken Sutherland

These books are available from all good bookshops or directly from Kogan Page Ltd, 120 Pentonville Road, London N1 9JN.
Tel: 0171 278 0433 Fax: 0171 837 6348

BUSINESS *ENTERPRISE*

DO YOUR OWN MARKET RESEARCH

THIRD EDITION

Paul N Hague
Peter Jackson

KOGAN
PAGE

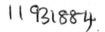

YOURS TO HAVE AND TO HOLD

BUT NOT TO COPY

First published in 1987
Second edition published in 1995
This edition published in 1998

Kogan Page Limited
120 Pentonville Road
London N1 9JN

British Library Cataloguing in Publication Data

A CIP record for this book is available from the British Library.

ISBN 0 7494 2652 7

Typeset by Kogan Page
Printed and bound in Great Britain by Clays Ltd, St Ives plc

Contents

Contents

Preface

We have spent nearly all our working lives in market research and largely (together) in a market research agency. We certainly believe that market research is a profession based on valid theory and constantly developing practice. Some of the techniques which have been developed are sophisticated and require long training and apprenticeship to become proficient in their application. However, we do not intend to overstate the extent to which mysteries and arcane skills are involved. Much market research is based on quite simple principles which can be rapidly understood and applied if coupled with a good measure of common sense. Similarly, although some market research projects require access to considerable re-sources and organisation (particularly for large scale interviewing programmes), many other information needs can be well met by the lone 'do your own' researcher.

So who might need to carry out 'do your own' market research? Almost anybody who is involved in making or helping to make marketing and similar sorts of decisions. This includes people such as:

- Owners and managers of smaller businesses.
- Sales and marketing staff of any size of business where there is no professional research staff in-house.
- A new recruit asked to carry out market research as an initial project.
- Staff or volunteers working in non-commercial organisations which need to take marketing type decisions – eg the potential for letting a new clubhouse as a contribution towards its construction costs.

Our book is written for this sort of reader; someone who needs to carry out practical market research without a two-year study programme. Possibly the research need is expected to be one-off or at most infrequent. Consequently, there is little theory in this book except where we believe it to be practically essential and even then the concepts are kept as simple as possible. Similarly, unlike more academic texts, there are few references apart from practical sources of information (given at the end of relevant chapters). There is, though, a short bibliography and we urge readers to follow up at least some of this further reading. We certainly do not want to leave the impression that one short book can communicate all that is important in market research. At most, we can hope to provide a good starting point.

Over the years we have read widely in our subject and have written several more specialised books. However, the foundation of *Do Your Own Market Research* is our experience of the many hundred projects carried out by our agency in almost all markets. We, therefore, owe foremost thanks to the companies for which we carried out these projects – our clients. We also wish to mention our many present and past colleagues whose ideas and good practice we have assimilated over the years.

Paul Hague
Peter Jackson

What Is Market Research?

Before discussing practical aspects of doing your own market research, some background understanding of the subject and why research is carried out is required. This is the purpose of this chapter. The topics covered include the need for information in marketing decision-making and what market research can provide, differences between markets and implications for market research, a very brief introductory outline of the market research process with signposts to other chapters and finally when and where 'do your own' market research is practical (and when it is not).

RESEARCH FOR MARKETING DECISIONS

The purpose of market research is to assist and improve marketing decisions. In any field, the basis of good decision-making is having effective information available and using it. This applies throughout business including finance, production, and personnel, as well as marketing, and is also equally true for non-commercial organisations. Almost any information required in marketing decisions and the methods used to acquire that information can be considered to be market research, but as a distinct and specialised activity, it is the provision of information about the market which is usually the central concern.

If marketing is about the profitable satisfaction of market needs, we clearly have to understand our markets and the needs of consumers – individuals or organisations – that make up these markets. This understanding can be intuitive and based on common sense and many successful decisions have been and are based on no more than hunches. However, in competitive markets where implementing a decision may require major financial resources (what is major is relative to the size of a business) and where the costs of failure are high, there is a need for decision-making based on more rigorous and reliable data. The techniques of market research can deliver this increased confidence and so reduce some of the risks.

The scope of market research can be introduced by thinking about just one sort of marketing decision – what to do about a product that is producing below-average or unsatisfactory profits. Regardless of the product, there are in fact only three possible options, in isolation or combination: sell more, charge more or cut costs. Table 1.1 illustrates some (but not an exhaustive list) of the information, potentially available through market research, which might be required before deciding on how to improve these profits. In each case the information concerns an understanding of the market and the consumers making up the market. If the profits are to be increased through selling more (raising extra revenue) there must be an opportunity to achieve this, and some questions that may need answering include:

- Is the market in total or in specific segments big enough to provide the extra sales?
- What share of the market is already held? The larger this is, the harder it may be to gain extra volume.
- Are there some barriers to achieving extra sales which will have to be addressed: poor distribution, low consumer awareness or possibly the product not matching many consumers' needs?

Table 1.1 *Marketing strategies and relevant information to increase the profitability of a product*

Strategy	Marketing Information
Sell more	Size of the total market for the product
	Breakdown of the market by segment
	Existing share held
	Availability of the product – eg retail penetration
	Consumer awareness of the product
	Consumer acceptance of the product
Charge more	Competitive pricing levels
	Price sensitivity of the market
	Consumer perception of the value of the product
	Likely effect on consumer demand of price increase
Cut costs	Whether any resulting product re-formulation would influence consumer perceptions of the product.

For the other strategies to increase profitability, relevant questions also need answering before a decision can be confidently made.

Whilst in this book the emphasis is on market research for marketing decisions, the techniques of market research are also widely applicable in other areas. Some examples include opinion polls (used for political marketing), social issues and policy-making, and personnel management (eg employee attitude surveys).

MARKETS AND MARKET RESEARCH

Market research can be applied in any type of market. However, depending on the nature of the market there are differences in approach and technique. Anyone planning to do their own market research will be primarily interested in the approach needed in their own area: even full-time professional researchers tend to specialise in markets as well as research techniques. The most fundamental division of markets is between those where the consumers are individuals or households buying for their own needs and satisfaction and those where the consuming unit is an organisation – a business, a public authority or other body. In such cases individuals may make the decision and act for the organisation but it is not (or should not be) individual and personal needs that are being satisfied.

In consumer markets, the number of potential buyers of a product is often a significant proportion of a total population and therefore running into millions. Techniques used to research these markets include quantitative methods based on rigorous sampling as well as qualitative techniques, which probe the complex consumer perceptions and motivations which provide the dynamics to these markets. Consumer markets can be further sub-divided, particularly between fmcgs (fast moving consumer goods – food and similar frequent purchases) and other markets – media, travel and leisure, financial, consumer durables, etc. FMCGs, in particular, are also retail markets and anyone marketing through retail distribution needs to know as much about what is happening in the shops as among final consumers.

Some aspects of consumer market research are very specialised and require either skills or resources which effectively rule out a 'do your own' approach – the research must be bought in. However, simple market research projects can be effectively carried out even in sophisticated fmcg sectors. And what is simple in terms of research techniques may be adequate or even better than over-complication.

Any market where the consuming unit is an organisation requires different market research techniques, or at least a change of emphasis. For one thing the decision-making process is often complex with different groups in the organisation involved, each with distinct concerns (eg the production, technical, purchasing and financial departments may all influence decisions for engineering products). Also the structure of the markets are very different, often with a few companies accounting for the majority of the demand for the product or service. At one time, markets made up of organisations were referred to as 'industrial', but now it is common to speak of a separate business-to-business sector. These are markets where, although the consumers are organisations, their numbers are typically large. Often the products are for the office rather than the factory floor. Examples include equipment such as computers, copiers and franking machines and also services such as telecommunications and financial. In research terms, the main point about these business-to-business markets is that the methods developed for consumer markets, including large-scale and structured interviewing of statistically valid samples, can be, and are, applied.

The category 'industrial market' now tends to be applied in a more restrictive sense to products and services used in manufacturing production. Often, these are also technical products requiring, on the part of anyone carrying out market research, at least an appreciation of the underlying principles. Also the methods used are different, reflecting that these are often small markets in terms of consuming units – eg a dozen carefully selected interviews may cover organisations accounting for 75 per cent of the market. This small scale allows one researcher with no or very limited assistance to carry out, on a 'do your own' basis, a wider range of market research than is often possible in large-number consumer or business-to-business markets. Also, the 'do your own' researcher with a technical understanding of the market and products may have some advantages over the 'professional' researcher.

Markets, whether consumer, industrial or business-to-business, are not confined to single countries. Increasingly, marketing is international including global brands or marketing programmes. Various economic and political considerations are bringing about these changes including GATT and, for the UK, membership of the single market of the European Union. In some markets it will be increasingly the case that the scope is at least the whole of Europe and the research need accordingly will be international. Confining the research to the

UK alone may be in future as parochial as now restricting it to, say, Lancashire. In both consumer and industrial/business-to-business markets the techniques are basically the same whether the UK or the whole EU is covered in a market research project. However, there are some obvious differences of detail, not least of which is language. Also the practicalities of carrying out specific types of research in the relatively homogenous EU area, let alone in less developed areas, need to be thought about.

International research is not beyond the practical scope of a 'do your own' approach; multi-country desk research, for example, can often be carried out in the UK and even an international programme of interviewing can be considered. However, the complexities of international research and some of the skills and resources needed may often require at least some of the required information to be bought-in.

THE SCOPE OF MARKET RESEARCH INFORMATION

Regardless of the market, the types of decisions that need to be taken tend to be similar. Whether the product is a confectionery bar or engineering equipment, the marketing plan needs to cover areas such as the product specification and its relation to consumer needs and requirements, branding, pricing, distribution methods, advertising support, market definition and segmentation, forecast sales levels, etc. Each of these decisions requires information from the market to increase the chance of getting it right. Common information requirements met through market research are listed below, although this list is by no means exhaustive. Also no single research commission would cover all or even most areas. As argued later, research that is focused and restricted to what is really crucial to the decision is more likely to be effective.

Table 1.2 *Common information areas met through market research*

The Market	Market Structure
Total market size	Major players – shares held
Consumer profiles and requirements	Branding – shares held
Market segmentation	Distribution structure
Trends – growing, declining	Trends in positions held

Consumer Perceptions

Underlying needs
Perceptions of brands
Perceptions of suppliers and
    brands
Perceptions of suppliers and
    retailers

New Product Development

Unsatisfied product needs
    (gap analysis)
Acceptance of new products
Communication of new
    products
New product branding

Distribution/Retailing

Distribution levels achieved
Sales at retail level and by
    type of outlet
Retailer requirements

Advertising and Promotion

Campaign planning
Creative development
Promotion evaluation
Sales activity planning
Media data

Brands

Positioning
Profiling – strengths and
    weaknesses
Valuation – what is the added
    value?

Products

Analysis of available products
Product usage and consumption
    patterns
Product differentiation
Product linkage to market and
    market segmentation
Product innovation and life cycle
Consumer satisfaction with
    products and service support

Pricing

Current pricing structures
Past trends
Price sensitivity
Predicted effects of price changes

Although each information area is potentially a requirement in all markets, the characteristics of specific markets mean that there is considerable variation in the detailed coverage sought in each case. Market segmentation, for example, means something rather different for fmcgs than for engineering components. Similarly, in industrial markets there is often a greater need for understanding the structure of suppliers and their organisation, whilst in consumer markets branding issues are often a far greater concern.

One important classification of market research information, regardless of the type of market, is quantitative and qualitative information. *Quantitative* research is concerned with measurement of a market and includes market size, the size of market segments, brand shares, purchase frequencies, awareness measures of brands, distribution levels, etc. Such quantitative data are required to some level of accuracy (though not in all cases to very high levels) and the methods used must be capable of achieving this. In consumer markets at least, quantitative information is almost always based on extrapolating from a sample of the general population or market, and the sampling methods must be sufficiently rigorous to allow this.

Qualitative information is rather harder to define but the emphasis is on 'understanding' rather than simple measurement – advert A is recalled better than Advert B (quantitative information), but *how* does A work as an advert and *why* is it more effective than B? Much qualitative research is concerned with empathising with the consumer and establishing the meanings *he or she* attaches to products, brands and other marketing objects. Another focus is motivation – eg why does one product rather than another meet consumer needs and what are these needs that are being met? As with quantitative information, qualitative research is conducted among a sample, in this case usually a small one since there is no attempt to extrapolate in any rigorous way from the total population. In the case of attitudes to brands, for example, it will be considered adequate to be confident that a particular attitude syndrome exists to some extent among the population rather than seeking to say whether 10 per cent or 20 per cent of the population have these attitudes. Quantitative and qualitative information is complementary, and a particular marketing decision may call for both sorts (the information areas in Table 1.2 include quantitative and qualitative). Furthermore, quantitative information may require 'exploratory' qualitative research to be carried out so that the particular measures can be defined meaningfully.

The practicality of 'do your own' market research is linked to the type of information sought. Some types of information require specialised techniques and resources (eg retail audit research). However, generally, most types of information can be covered in some respects or to some extent without buying-in the services of a professional research agency.

THE MARKET RESEARCH PROCESS

The collection of any facts relevant to a marketing decision can be considered as market research. However, we are concerned with something rather more than an occasional and haphazard use of snippets. A formal definition of the market research process can be as follows:

> *Market Research* – the systematic collection, analysis and interpretation of information relevant to marketing decisions.

Market research can be carried out as a one-off project to meet a specific requirement – eg whether or not to enter a new market – and this is called *ad hoc* research, or it can involve continuous or regular tracking – eg to monitor the market share held by a product or brand. Do your own market research is more likely to be *ad hoc* but the basic process is much the same in either case and is illustrated in Figure 1.1.

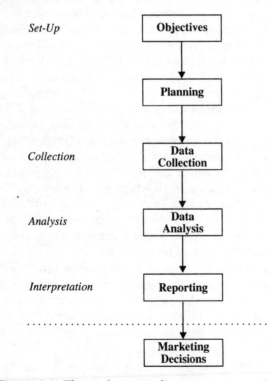

Figure 1.1 *The market research process*

The starting point of any market research project is to define objectives. If this is not done adequately, nearly all the effort put into the work will be wasted. Objectives are a statement of why the research is being carried out and links to what information is being sought. This subject is developed in Chapter 2. A plan of how this objective is to be met and how the information is to be obtained is then required. The resources needed (including money) and the timescale involved also need to be considered. Where *ad hoc* research is commissioned from a professional agency, the plan is virtually always documented in the form of a research proposal. It is recommended that even if the research is carried out on a 'do your own' basis by the person who will use the information, a written plan in some form is prepared before work starts in earnest. Research planning is also discussed in the next chapter.

Data collection is often the visible part of market research – the interviewer in the shopping mall pestering time-pressed shoppers to answer 'just a few questions'. Data collection is a vital part of the whole process but it is a mistake to think of it as the same as market research – all the other parts of the process are also vital. There are various types and techniques of data collection, with the most fundamental division between desk (secondary) research and field-work (primary) research. The practicalities of these approaches are covered in several later chapters; desk research in Chapter 3 and fieldwork in Chapters 4 to 8.

Fieldwork normally involves interviewing and completing a questionnaire for each individual or organisation in the sample. This may number tens, hundreds or even thousands (but not in a 'do your own' project). The individual questionnaires and responses are usually of little or no interest; what is required is an aggregation of the whole sample or perhaps groupings within that sample. Data processing produces this.

Having produced an analysis and aggregation of the data (and this includes what is found through desk research) it needs interpreting and presenting in a meaningful way so that the decision-maker can act on the results. This is the reporting stage of the process and may involve the researcher making recommendations on policy. Both data processing and reporting are covered in Chapter 9.

The final step in the process is taking a decision, based on the research outcome, and acting on it. In 'do your own' projects the researcher and decision-maker may be one and the same but this does not have to be the case; the 'in-house' researcher may be working for an internal client. Surprisingly, quite a lot of research is not acted on and the time and money involved is wasted. This may be because the research results are not appropriate to the decisions being made and this is often the result of poor research design or planning. However, in other cases, usually involving bought-in rather than 'do your own' research, the results are ignored because they do not match preconceptions; the new product is 'obviously' a winner even though the research pointed to a mismatch with market need, the Company's service support is excellent and the dissatisfaction identified 'must be a sample fluke' or the new advertising is so creative that research 'just cannot capture its subtleties'. Occasionally hunches and guesses are better than hard facts but this is rare. If a decision has been made before research is carried out and is in practice not going to be changed, why bother with the research? Do not carry out market research and then ignore the findings.

'DO YOUR OWN' VERSUS BUYING-IN MARKET RESEARCH

This book is about 'do your own' market research. Often the research is done on this basis because the only alternative is no research. Self-help is almost always much cheaper than buying-in and especially if no or a low value is put on the researcher's time. For most smaller companies the costs of using professionals may well be out of the question. However, 'do your own' research is not just a matter of Hobson's choice; there can be some real advantages over buying-in. These include:

- The research can be exactly tailored to what is needed rather than what the research supplier thinks is needed or believes is wanted. As already stated and as will be discussed further, research planning is essential, but this does not exclude flexibility and a 'do your own' project can be shaped by initial findings. Contractual considerations usually limit the flexibility of bought-in research in this respect.
- The 'do your own' researcher may not be a market research expert but can have a far greater understanding of the background to a market or the technical aspects of products and applications. This is often true in industrial markets. The need for product and market knowledge can be overstated but bought-in research may be limited or deficient because the agency concerned is just not qualified in this sense.

- 'Do your own' research results may be understood much better; either because the user of the data has collected it or because the researcher has the empathy with the decision-maker that comes from working together long-term. It is one thing for a professional outside researcher to describe your customers' feelings towards your company and it is another if it were you who did all or most of the interviews. 'Do your own' research is immediate in a way that a bought-in service is not.

However, whatever the potential benefits of 'do your own' research, its limitations must also be recognised. Good research aids decision-making but if it is poorly done the output may be a lot worse than useless; it may be misleading. A good researcher recognises his or her limitations, recognises when the work needs to be bought-in and understands that if this is not economically practicable it may be better not to attempt any.

The limitations of 'do your own' research are mainly skills and resources. Some types of research involve technical skills, which may be lacking. This may be the case in much qualitative research and where more complex statistical techniques are needed – eg often in pricing research and complex segmentation studies. Another sort of skill deficiency in international research is language abilities.

Given time and determination even the more obscure skills of market research can be learnt (including through practice, which is as important as book-knowledge). However, 'do your own' research is nearly always constrained by resources. There is a practical limit to what one man or woman, even with some assistance, can take on. This applies particularly to fieldwork (desk research is nearly always a one-person activity). Small sample industrial market interviewing or qualitative consumer research is usually within the capabilities of a small team, particularly if the phone is used, but a nationwide or international sample of hundreds or thousands of respondents is obviously beyond practical capabilities.

There are also other reasons why bought-in market research may be necessary. This includes a possible need to influence an outside group (eg a source of finance) through using the credibility of independent research. You may be just as capable of doing the work well but the bank will give more weight to a report from Hague Jackson Marketing Ltd. Also, independent research can overcome or side-step internal politics. The new product may be a no-hoper but if it is the boss's baby let outsiders tell him the bad news.

Where, for whatever reason, research needs to be bought-in, there is a well-established market research 'industry' to supply the service. This is described in Chapter 10 together with guidance on how and what to buy. As will be described, there are various ways of buying-in research ranging from 'full service' where the whole project is off-loaded to 'field and tab' where just the parts of the process requiring extensive resources are purchased, leaving design and reporting in-house. There is also an enormous range of published and syndicated research to consider as an alternative to an *ad hoc* service.

Planning a Market Research Project

The 'do your own' researcher is often tempted to 'get researching' as soon as possible, particularly if he or she is also the eventual user of the research. However, as in most things, some initial planning pays off in the long run. The main elements in an effective research plan are summarised below and discussed in this chapter.

- The decisions to be made and problems to be solved.
- Research objectives.
- Information coverage.
- Accuracy levels.
- Research methods.
- Resources.
- Timetable.

INFORMATION FOR DECISION-MAKING

With very few exceptions, a market research project should contribute to marketing decision-making or to solving problems that will entail making decisions. Keeping to this principle throughout a project will avoid many problems. The output of the research may be interesting but it should not *just* be interesting; it should meet a relevance test – how can this be used to make a better decision.

Obviously the decisions which market research can guide are as varied as the businesses which take them. A few examples are:

- Should we seek to enter the Spanish market?
- Should money be spent (and how much) on developing a particular new product?

- Where should an additional distribution point be opened in the North?
- Which style of packaging should be used?

Such decisions will often entail linked or secondary decisions that the research may need to take into account. The decision to enter the Spanish market for example will also entail decisions about how to do this – which products to offer, how to distribute them, pricing, promotion methods, etc.

Sometimes a business is faced with an obvious problem but cannot initially see which decisions may have to be made, eg:

- Sales of a particular product are declining.
- New legislation will lead to higher unit costs but the market is believed to be increasingly competitive.

In such cases research may firstly be used to provide a diagnosis of the problem. However, if the research is well planned the outcome will also point to the decisions that need to be taken.

RESEARCH OBJECTIVES

Every research project should have a defined and explicit objective which succinctly states *why* the research is being carried out. All other aspects of planning and carrying out the research flow from this objective; in other words if they do not contribute towards achieving this objective they almost certainly should not be carried out. The objective should relate to the marketing decision which will have to be made or the problem that needs a solution (and decision), eg:

> Identify and quantify the opportunity for the Company to enter the Spanish market and provide information relevant to planning how to do this.

Research objectives should be brief and should not be confused with a listing of the information required to meet them (sometimes referred to as detailed objectives). Where the researcher is not the person responsible for making the decisions, it is essential that the objective is agreed with the 'client'; it is no use carrying out an extensive project and then discovering the marketing manager is considering entering the Portuguese as well as the Spanish market.

There is a certain art in drafting effective objectives and this is not just a matter of words – badly thought out objectives will lead to poor or less than optimum research. Two traps to avoid are the global, all-encompassing objectives and those which pre-judge the problem or decisions to be made. An example of a global and too ambitious objective might be:

Examine the place of the Company in the market place and identify new opportunities.

Where would the researcher start working to such an objective? It is hard to imagine anything useful coming out of this project.

Pre-judgement is the opposite of over-ambition. Assumptions are made which ought to be tested through research. Faced with falling sales, for example, the temptation may be to research customer acceptance of the product and its features. But quite possibly this is not the problem at all; maybe the distribution system just does not get the product to customers. Where the starting point for the research is a problem rather than a decision to be made, an effective approach is to think of and list as many explanations as possible. In other words develop alternate hypotheses. This may be done by the researcher but better still at a 'brain-storming' of all the key staff involved. With only a little effort the list of hypotheses is likely to be quite extensive and probably more than can be sensibly covered in the research project. In this case some selection will have to be made of the hypotheses which are to be tested in the research and this is likely to be on a judgement of which is the more likely explanation of the problem; evidence that is already available may enable some hypotheses to be confidently discounted. With this done the hypotheses which do seem worth testing will enable a valid research objective to be set.

INFORMATION COVERAGE

To meet the defined objective, a range of information will be required and will in turn be an input into the decisions eventually made. For a given objective the information list, with only a little thought, will soon be quite long, possibly too long. In the case of the 'Spanish' project for example, the information coverage list might be as follows:

Identify and quantify the opportunity for the Company to enter the Spanish market and provide information relevant to planning how to do this

1. The size of the market for the Company's products with break-down by:
   Product grouping
   Customer group
   Region.
2. Trends in market size over the last five years and prospects for the next five with breakdown as per 1.
3. Existing suppliers to the Spanish market, shares held with breakdowns as per 1.
4. Basis of competition between suppliers, eg product differentiation, service, pricing.
5. Pricing levels in the market; use of discounts, etc.
6. Distribution structures and links to primary suppliers.
7. Customer satisfaction with existing suppliers and their relative standing in the market. Any unsatisfied customer needs.

This list is by no means exhaustive and other information headings may also be considered important. There is no such thing as an absolute right or wrong coverage, although the effectiveness of the research will be shaped by what is included or left out; the list will be more or less useful. Often the problem is not so much that headings are left out, but that the coverage is too comprehensive in relation to the research resources available. The example given above for instance is likely to involve quite a major research project and it is very possible that the resources available are insufficient to cover all that seems useful. This is particularly likely to be the case for a smaller company and in 'do your own' research projects. The initial 'wish list' of headings may, therefore, need pruning or separating into what is absolutely vital to know and what is of lesser importance.

Another approach to meeting an objective that appears to entail an extensive research coverage and major research input is staging. In the above example of the Spanish market it is possible that coverage of the market size (without detailed breakdowns) and suppliers' shares may indicate a limited or nil opportunity of market entry. If this is the case, other information would be of no practical use. It may be sensible, therefore, to establish market size and suppliers' shares in a first-stage project and on the basis of the outcome to then decide whether further research is justified. Quite possibly this first-stage research can be carried out quickly and at low cost (eg through desk research). Staging is particularly advantageous in 'do your own' research. Even if there is no apparent basis for staging the information coverage, we would usually recommend carrying out desk research before planning any fieldwork. This is discussed shortly.

A final aspect of defining the information coverage is to set boundaries to the research. These may be geographical (eg the market in Great Britain excluding Northern Ireland), by product range (eg high density polystyrene) or by market or application (eg use in the construction industry, for trade use, etc). Again these boundaries should be explicit and agreed with the 'client'. As in other aspects of coverage, it may be necessary to compromise from the ideal wish list.

A well-defined research coverage will not only make for more effective research but is also very useful when questionnaires are designed; much of the work is effectively already done.

ACCURACY

If professional market researchers ask their clients how accurate any data should be, the answer is often 'very accurate' or 'as accurate as possible'. However, accuracy, at least where fieldwork is involved, has a price, and as a general rule increases in accuracy not only cost more but cost disproportionately more*.

A high level of accuracy is not always needed to meet the overall research objective. If in the Spanish example the company would consider sales of £500,000 pa to be worthwhile, it really would not matter if the total market size was £40 million or £50 million (an accuracy of ± 25 per cent). However, in other cases a more closely defined level of accuracy may be essential to meet the research objectives. If, for example, in an advertising research study, the objective was to measure the impact of a campaign on brand awareness by comparing before and after campaign measures of awareness, the accuracy must be at least commensurate with the anticipated increase in awareness. If this is 10 per cent, a sampling

---

*   If a sample of 500 is statistically likely to be accurate to ± 5%, what size of sample will be needed to increase the accuracy to ± 2.5%? It is not 1000 but nearer 2000 and the costs involved possibly more than twice as high. Diminishing returns very much apply.

method with results at the two measurement stages of ± 5 per cent accuracy would not be capable of yielding reliable evidence on the effectiveness of the campaign since this accuracy level might imply an awareness level before the campaign of between 35 and 45 per cent if the sample result was 40 per cent and between 45 and 55 per cent after the campaign if the sample result was 50 per cent. In other words the data might imply that the campaign was very successful or that it had no effect at all.

In much research, however, precise definition of accuracy levels is not practically possible. Even so, some judgement should be made on the necessary reliability of the information provided. This may be as simple as a contrast between an attempt at measurement (quantitative research) and just description and explanation (qualitative research). Both approaches can contribute to effective marketing decisions but it is important that neither is used for the wrong application. Like information coverage, accuracy levels need to be considered before deciding on appropriate research methods.

RESEARCH METHODS

Research methods are concerned with how the required information will be collected, and effective planning presupposes an understanding of the alternatives, and how and when each can be effectively used. Chapters 3 to 8 cover these methods in more detail.

The most fundamental choice in research methods is between secondary or desk research and primary research or fieldwork. As we will show in the next chapter, the potential and scope of desk research is enormous and the objectives of many research projects undertaken on a 'do your own' basis can be largely or wholly met by this method. True, there is often some uncertainty of the outcome of desk research – what will be found or not. Also there are some types of information that in principle cannot be obtained in this way (eg usually attitude-type data such as how a particular company is regarded in its market-place). But, in general, we strongly advocate carrying out an initial desk research stage in 'do your own' projects before planning any other work. The reason for this is that desk research is nearly always far cheaper (and quicker) than primary research/fieldwork and there is no point in spending time and money interviewing to find out what is already available and accessible at little cost. In this respect 'do your own' research has an edge over buying-in on a full service basis. For various commercial reasons, market research agencies are unlikely to offer a desk research-only stage.

Once desk research is completed and, assuming it does not yield all the information required for the project, primary research or fieldwork can be planned to fill in the gaps. The choices involved – the elements of the research design – include the following issues (these are expanded in Chapter 4):

Decisions in primary research design

- The universe to be covered, eg: all adults, housewives, buyers of specific products in consumer markets and comparable aspects of industrial markets.
- Sectors or sub-groupings of the whole universe that are of specific interest and need to be considered in sampling design.
- The nature of the information sought and especially whether it is quantitative or qualitative.
- Sampling method and size (number of interviews).
- Method of interview – face to face, phone, postal, etc.

The basis of the decisions made in each of the above areas should relate to the research objectives, the planned information coverage and the accuracy sought. At least this should be so in theory. In practice other factors have to be taken into account and especially the resources available including the budget. Quite possibly the ideal may be face-to-face interviews with a sample of 250 decision-makers in consuming industries, but for practical reasons a postal survey has to be used instead. In commercial market research such compromises are inevitable whether the project is carried out on a 'do your own' basis or bought-in; research methods are seldom to a theoretical optimum and may fall well short of the ideal. However, there is some point beyond which compromises are a danger; if the affordable or practical methods are not capable of yielding the required data to adequate accuracy levels it will be better not to do the research at all; decisions based on hunches may be better than using fatally flawed and spurious research.

RESOURCES

As just suggested, research methods are inevitably determined by available resources and this is largely a matter of money; with enough cash, any shortcomings in existing resources can usually be overcome.

What budget should be made available for the research project? The methodologically pure researcher would argue that the budget should be whatever is needed to meet the research objectives, to provide the information required and to finance the methods needed to produce that information to the defined accuracy level. However, in practice it is more a question of what funds are available or can be afforded for the project relative to other calls on business expenditure. Furthermore, even if cash is freely available, there are other considerations, especially the amount at risk in the decision which the research is to guide. If the decision may entail capital expenditure of £1 million, a research budget of £10,000 may be well worth spending – if the planned expenditure appears to be a poor investment only the research cost will be lost rather than most of the £1 million. However, if the decision has a much lower cost (say £10,000) the value of doing the research will be less; obviously do not spend £10,000 on research to decide whether to invest in a project entailing only this level of expenditure.

However it is done, research planning should, therefore, include making a budget available for the work. Monitoring of actual expenditure against this budget should then be carried out so that it is kept to, or at least only exceeded for good reasons. In a 'do your own' project, the true costs include both the real and the notional. The former includes items such as travel costs and materials, whilst the latter is the cost of the researcher's time. Assuming he or she is in paid employment, this time has a cost and if there is a diversion from other work, it is the 'opportunity' cost that matters – revenue lost from not doing routine or normal work. It all depends on the systems and culture of the organisation whether or not such notional costs are identified, measured and set against the research activity, and we would not suggest that this should necessarily be done. However, costing in this way does allow a true comparison to be made with buying-in the work as an alternative to 'do your own'. Buying-in research can be the cheaper option.

One other aspect of budgeting is the availability of grants from government or quasi-government bodies. Various agencies, for example the DTI (Department of Trade and Industry), make grants available to businesses and, in some cases, cover market research. Local TECs and Business Links are also worth contacting. Generally, any such grant has to be at least matched by the recipient and is more often given to meet the costs of outside services rather than the expense of internal staff. However, the schemes on offer change, and rather than go into further details here we suggest making contact with a local DTI office.

Apart from a cash budget, the major resource required for a research project is people. Who is available for the work and the time they can set aside affects not only how quickly the project can be carried out but also the methods which can be practically used. One 'do your own' researcher can realistically carry out a programme of, say, 20 key decision-maker interviews (in an industrial market) or a limited number of in-depth, qualitative interviews (in a consumer market) but they probably cannot even contemplate a nationwide visit programme to 100 respondents. Such limitations may necessitate a switch to other methods such as phone or post, or force a reduction in sample size (but with thought given to the effect on accuracy levels). To boost full-time resources, part-time and temporary staff can be drafted in from elsewhere in the Company or from outside, though this may lead to its own problems. Using the salesforce as an interviewing team for example is often a mistake; either the work is done unwillingly or in a biased way since good salesmen have different qualities than those needed by effective interviewers. Rather than using untrained temporary staff in this way, it may be better and more cost effective to buy-in some services from a professional research agency – eg on a 'field and tab' basis. This alternative is explored in Chapter 10.

Apart from money and people, 'do your own' market research requires little in the way of tangible resources. A car is likely to be needed and nowadays a PC is usually thought of as essential. Most businesses, however, will have both of these in place. The remaining essential is of course some skill in market research, which comes from learning the principles of the subject (eg from this book) and from practice, for which there is no quick substitute.

TIMETABLE

A research plan needs a timetable. Even if there is neither a real deadline nor constraint on the input, it is better to be committed to a finish date otherwise the project is likely to drag on forever. The two determinates of a timetable are the deadline and how long the planned research activities will take to carry out. Resources determine the latter and experience of the intended methods will enable realistic estimates to be made of how long each stage will take. In later chapters we give some indications of the timescales for various research methods. The deadline on the other hand is likely to be driven by external events and time-frames; the research results may be needed to fit the lead time in installing plant, or by the time the next year's business plan is developed, or by the end of an accounting period. To an extent it may be possible to speed up the research to fit such exterior constraints, or the method itself may be trimmed. Certainly good research can be carried out within a short timetable but beyond some point quality will be compromised. Some deadlines have to be met but many are not as fixed as they are made out to be.

For a substantial project, a formal written timetable should be prepared with the time span of each stage indicated. Figure 2.1 provides an example.

Activity	Dates
Commission	End October/early November
Briefing/draft questionnaire	Early to mid November
Pilot, interim meeting, draft and agree main questionnaire, translate where necessary	Mid November to early December
Full interview programme	Mid December to mid January
Analysis	Mid to end January
Presentation	End January/early February
Report	Mid February

Figure 2.1 *Example of a research timetable*

PREPARING A WRITTEN PLAN

We recommend that a formal written plan for the research should always be prepared that covers each aspect of the work discussed in this chapter. This may seem over formal where the researcher and user are one and the same, but even in this case efficient research is more likely if an explicit plan is drawn up. In such a case its format is immaterial and as long as it is legible, neatness and presentation quality carry no premium. Where the plan is to be presented to others, such as an internal client – perhaps before the budget is sanctioned – presentational quality is important. The message may be exactly the same, but high standards will enhance credibility. Where an outside agency is used for any part of the work, a plan in the form of a written proposal is standard practice.

3

Desk Research

Desk research is the process of accessing secondary research data – information collected for some other purposes than meeting the objectives of the particular project. The 'desk' may be in a library but increasingly it is a PC providing a gateway to cyber-data. The range of marketing information which can be obtained through desk research is vast and capable of meeting most of the data needs of many market research projects, especially those likely to be carried out on a 'do your own' basis. Moreover, for the 'do your own' researcher, desk research is a very practical tool – in most cases he or she is not at any disadvantage compared to the resources of a professional agency.

RESOURCES

Until the advent of on-line databases, access to libraries was the only important resource needed to carry out desk research. Despite the marvels of the information highway, some data are easier to access from hard copy and off the library shelves. All major cities have at least one good municipal or university library and few researchers will be more than an hour's travel from such a resource. There are also some important national libraries open to a desk researcher including a range of services from the *British Library*[1] and two important government resources – the *Central Statistical Office*[2] and the *DTI Export Marketing Information Centre*[3] – a major source in international market research. There are also very many specialist libraries run by industry bodies and others; these can best be located through *ASLIB*[4].

The modern alternative to hours spent in libraries is accessing databases on-line and the Internet. The tools needed to do this are a PC linked to a modem and communications software. Assuming a PC is already owned, the additional cost of going on-line is a few hundred pounds and anyone carrying out desk research with any frequency will want to use this route sooner or later.

THE INTERNET

The Internet is a global interconnection of networks that link servers (computers housing information) which in turn are connected to academic institutions, businesses, trade associations, government agencies, medical facilities, scientific establishments and private individuals. Using browsers such as Microsoft's Internet Explorer or Netscape's Navigator, it is possible to access the sites or user groups of the many millions who are now linked through the Net.

Accessing the Internet requires the user to have a computer with a modem and a subscription to a service provider such as America On Line (AOL), Demon or BT Internet. Thereafter it is a matter of dialling up the service provider to log on to the Internet and the payment of a local telephone charge. For market researchers, the Internet has two important sources of information:

1. the sites which companies, organisations and individuals have created to promote or communicate their products, services or views
2. user groups that are made up of people who have an interest in a particular subject.

Web sites are recognised by the prefix www. Companies operating in the UK typically have sites with citations such as www.company-name.co.uk., while those aiming at an international audience are more likely to be referenced as www.companyname.com.

Searching for information on a subject or a company through web sites is made easy by the many search engines that simply require an appropriate word string to find all references. Popular search engines such as Alta Vista, Yahoo or those that combine various engines such as WebCrawler, list the references in declining order of appropriateness to the search request.

A search strategy with a suitable arrangement of words may well hit the bull's eye and locate precisely the information that is being sought. More often the search will start a trail that follows the links between related sites. Thinking laterally is certainly the first principle of desk research using the Internet. The searcher must learn to surf from one site to another, book-marking those that are useful for downloading or copying into a work file.

There are over 10,000 user groups (also called news groups or discussion groups) on the Internet covering almost every subject. They are roughly organised by topic, ranging from hobbies and recreation (prefixed by rec) through to computers (comp), science (sci), and culture, religion, as well as 'alternative' subjects (alt). A question posted within an appropriate user group by a researcher may well find an answer from one of the millions of Internet users. An easy way to access user groups is through a search engine such as Deja News.

ON-LINE DATABASES

Databases of articles and reports, held on servers throughout the world, can easily be searched using a computer and modem. Some databases can now be accessed very cheaply via the Internet. However, much of the information required in market research is available from commercial providers who charge significantly for access either as an up-front figure or on a pay as you use basis – eg *MAID/Profound*[5], *Dialog/Datastar*[6], and *FT Profile*[7]. The user of such sources needs to become a subscriber and learn how to carry out searches efficiently (to minimise costs); free or low-cost training is offered to new subscribers.

The major benefit of any sort of on-line database is the speed of locating material through using techniques such as key-word searching and other methods that match what is available to what is sought. This is particularly of benefit in searching press files (looking through the last few months' issues of even one paper manually is a daunting task). However, it should be remembered that generally on-line databases are a means of accessing sources and not a source as such. Nearly everything available on-line can be obtained from traditional paper sources and in some cases this is the easier route. On-line database searching also needs skills which take time to learn and for this reason the occasional re-searcher may be better off using others to carry out database searches – several organisations including the British Library offer such a service (at a charge).

OTHER RESOURCES

Some other resources to mention as well as libraries and on-line databases include other forms of electronic media, buying publications and collecting free material.

Material such as abstracts, statistics and large directories are increasingly available on disk or CD-ROM and often on a subscription basis with regular updates. Where such a source is going to be consulted frequently, such formats may be the best way of accessing data. Searching and abstracting data is as convenient as on-line and once the initial cost is met (this may be substantial but often no more than buying traditional hard copy versions) there is no marginal cost of access (unlike pay-as-you-use on-line databases). CD-ROM in particular looks set to be an increasingly important format for researchers.

There is a very wide range of marketing research reports and other data for sale from numerous publishers and providers. However, this type of resource will be discussed in more detail in Chapter 10. The charges made for bought-in reports and similar sources range from the nominal to levels comparable to commissioning ad hoc research.

The final resource to mention is the opportunity to collect free information. Examples include product literature – particularly relevant in business and industrial markets – and accounts and reports from publicly quoted companies. With ingenuity, many other free data sources can be found.

INFORMATION SOURCES

In only one chapter in a short book it is not possible to give more than the briefest indication of the range of sources available for market research or indicate the scope of what can be found. Anyone intent on seriously developing desk research skills is urged to read wider*. Some major types of sources, however, include the following.

Government statistics

In most projects 'hard' statistical data will be sought and no desk researcher will go far without using UK government statistics. These cover most areas of business and social life, although in recent years there has been some contraction in scope. The *Annual Abstract Of Statistics*[8] is an easy way into the major series. There is also a free catalogue of the main publications (from the Government Book-

---

*　A useful next step may be to read *Desk Research* by Peter Jackson. See Bibliography.

shop, HMSO) which is well worth picking up, but the bible is the *Guide To Official Statistics*[9], a substantial volume which is regularly revised.

The UK government is not of course unique in providing a statistical service. Governments of most developed countries provide as good or better data covering their own territories – the USA for example is very well documented. There are also international bodies collecting and publishing statistics. For the EU the office responsible is *Eurostat*[10] and this source will increasingly be important in projects covering the whole single market of the EU. Two other major publishers are the *UN*[11] and the *OECD*[12].

As with other sources, government statistics can increasingly be accessed on-line as well as from hard copy. Data-Star is one on-line host providing access.

Trade and industry bodies

Every trade, no matter how obscure, nearly always has some collective body to represent its interests (and also usually spawns several trade publications – see below). To meet members' needs and for PR purposes most of these bodies publish or can make available (sometimes to members only) considerable information about their industry. The organisation and sophistication of these bodies and the volume of the information offered varies enormously. Some do no more than publish an annual report, whilst others are the recognised source of detailed industry statistics (eg the *SMMT*[13] for the motor vehicle industry). There are various directories of these organisations (eg *Directory of British Associations*[14]) and a desk researcher should not only seek out publications of relevant bodies but also contact them directly; information which is not published may be obtained in this way.

Market research reports

This type of source is also discussed in Chapter 10. It is enough for now to know that there are over 30,000 such reports available, located through several sources (eg *Market Search*[15] and *Findex*[16]).

The press

The general, business and trade press are key sources for the desk researcher. As well as 'news', these sources include much background material including special supplements on industries and markets. The general press includes the quality dailies and Sundays

– *The Times, Independent, Guardian, Telegraph,* etc and periodicals such as *The Economist.* Of the business press, *The Financial Times*[17] is a major reference source in its own right. Although there are several press indexes (eg *Research Index*[18]) available, searching the general press is now better done on-line using a host such as FT Profile. This allows rapid access to material by subject and keyword.

In industrial markets especially, the trade press is a very important market research source. Every industry and trade has regular journals which can be identified in publications such as *BRAD*[19] and *Pims*[20]. Whilst much useful data is in these sources, finding material can be quite laborious. Many publications have a poor or no index and some are not available – even in abstract – on-line; there may be no alternative to reading through hard copy back issues.

Directories

Directories provide details of organisations involved in markets as suppliers or in other roles, and are the usual source for preparing the specialised samples used in industrial market research. Details for profiling individual companies can also be found. There are broadly two classes of directories: the general and the specialised. The former cover most or all industries and include *Kompass*[21] and *Key British Enterprises*[22]. These sources are in all commercial sections of libraries and are published in CD-ROM as well as traditional bound form. The databases on which they are based are also available on-line in some cases and entries can be abstracted to meet complex criteria (industry, size of business, area, etc). As well as such general directories, there are also publications covering specific industries, usually in more detail. Often these are published by the same organisations as the trade press. Specialised directories can be located through guides such as *Current British Directories*[23].

Company accounts

To profile individual players in a market and sometimes to estimate market size, company accounts can be a vital source. In the UK these must be filed each year at Companies House*. Copies of filed accounts can be obtained direct from *Companies House*[24], although

---

* Smaller companies need file only limited information and this can reduce the value of this source in niche markets.

in practice it is often easier to take the details from summary publications such as *ICC*[25] or *EXTEL*[26] – the latter for quoted companies. Agents, eg *Circare*[27], can also be used to carry out searches at Companies House and this service can be quite cheap. Company data, including for overseas companies, can also be accessed on-line, eg from *Jordans*[28].

THE RANGE OF INFORMATION AVAILABLE

Sources such as those outlined above can be used to obtain data on the large majority of subjects likely to be covered in a market research project. These include those mentioned below.

The marketing environment

Markets do not exist in isolation and are shaped by environmental factors such as the state of the general economy, demographic trends, the legislative framework and various social factors. An understanding of these external factors is likely to be part of any full analysis of a market. The marketing environment is generally well documented and desk research (rather than primary research) is the only practical source available. The economy, demographics and key social variables are all well covered by the government's statistical service and the many publications it produces. Other sources in this area include special reports (government and private) and press commentary.

Market structure and size

The structure of most business and industrial markets can be fully analysed through desk research. Sources include the general and trade press, directories, company financial data, published reports, trade association output and government statistics. The latter source includes *UK Markets* (formerly *Business Monitor*)[29] which provides, for all industries, details of production, imports and exports with detailed product breakdowns on an annual basis. Government statistics such as *UK Markets* go back into long time series and provide a basis for historical and future trend analysis. This source or others may not provide market size estimates of the specific category of interest, but with ingenuity reasonable approximations can usually be arrived at from top-down (making estimates from a wider classification which includes the one of interest) or bottom-up (aggregating sub-classifications). The skill in this sort of work includes bringing together disparate pieces of data from separate sources, eg *UK Markets* plus press reports and company accounts analysis. A useful additional type of source to mention for market sizing and analysis is various compendiums such as *Market Assessment of Top Markets*[30] and *Market Size Digest*[31].

Suppliers and brands

Data on suppliers and brands can be thought of as an extension of the sort of market structure analysis considered above and may include profiles of major suppliers and their brands, marketing methods and advertising tactics, and factors making for success. The press (including trade journals), directories, company accounts and published reports are all potentially useful sources. So is advertising and trade literature (especially in technical markets) and such material can usually be collected free. One important area of information which is usually outside the scope of desk research is consumers' attitudes to and satisfaction with suppliers. Generally this can only be obtained through primary research, although in some industries published reports may have relevant data.

Distribution and retailing

Although in specialised industrial markets, supply may be direct between manufacturer and consumer, most business markets have a distribution structure in place including importers, main distributors, local dealers, etc. Sources to provide an analysis of these structures are much the same as just discussed for primary suppliers. Consumer markets are generally retail markets and retailing generally is very well documented including in the press and published reports.

Products

Desk research can enable detailed product information to be built up and analysed. In some markets various publications compare, feature by feature, what is available on the market. Mail order catalogues are another source of product details. Product literature is often particularly relevant in technical markets and is a source for analysing product features. Visits to exhibitions and trade fairs to collect this literature is an example of 'near' desk research which can be used before moving into primary research.

Pricing information may also be available from the sources just mentioned, although the difference between list prices and what is actually paid may lessen the value of such information.

Desk research is not usually thought to have a role in new product evaluation and certainly consumer reaction to a new product has to be established through primary research. However, the fate of other new launches in a particular market can provide very useful information and this can be accessed from the trade press and other sources.

International marketing

The relative economy of desk research is even more pronounced in international marketing with libraries and on-line databases, accessible in the UK, meeting many of the information needs to guide overseas marketing. The types of sources available and the range of topics is much the same as those in the UK. However, the consistency and comparability of data is often a problem. For the EU markets there are a number of pan-Europe sources including the output from Eurostat, which has already been mentioned. Many published reports are also international in scope.

LOCATING DATA

The major problem in carrying out desk research is not the availability of data as much as locating it. One approach is to simply browse on the library shelves and hope to find something useful. It is true that in some projects this is how a vital piece of information is actually found, but, in general, a more systematic approach is needed.

Because of the demand to locate marketing information, a number of publishers produce and regularly up-date 'sources of sources'. These include *The UK Marketing Source Book*[32] and *The Source Book*[33]. These cover organisations providing information and on-line data as well as listing conventional publications. Various classification methods and indexing can be used to find relevant subjects and the references can then be followed up. There are also other general guides which can be used to track down sources of data including those covering published research, the press, directories and statistics – examples of all of these have been mentioned above. For international markets there are comparable 'sources of sources' including *The Guide*[34], *European Directory of Marketing Information*[35] and *Directory of International Sources of Business Information*[36]. Some or all of these 'sources of sources' will be found in a good library together with other indexes, eg *Research Index* for the press. The library's own cataloguing and indexing systems also provide a means of systematically searching out data. With experience, sources likely to be relevant to a particular field will become familiar and provide short-cuts, although a full search technique is recommended as well.

Another means of locating data sources is through direct contact with organisations and individuals having knowledge of a particular field. Trade associations and the publishers of information are examples. This sort of approach strays outside desk research in the strictest sense but such contacts and a two-way traffic between sources (which identifies potential contacts) and informal interviewing (to identify sources) is a means of getting the most value from desk research at little extra cost (possibly a saving if sources are identified more efficiently).

Apart from easy access, the key benefit of on-line databases is the ability to search for and locate data. There is some skill involved and 'search strategies' are needed to get the most out of access and keep costs down. However, this begs the question of which database should be accessed in the first place – no one 'host' provides a direct gateway to all cyber-data. To fill the gap there are a number of database source books published including *On Line Business and Company Databases*[37] and *Directory of On Line Databases*[38] – the latter having a US slant. The major hosts (eg *FT Profile*, *Data-Star*) also publish their own guides. Lastly there is the very effective concept of 'surfing the net' – using direct access to the worldwide Internet to find data, as briefly covered on page 25.

PLANNING, RECORDING AND EVALUATING DESK RESEARCH

To efficiently search for data, a plan is needed, especially for a project of any size. In Chapter 2 the general need to plan research and put the plan down on paper was urged. A written plan also applies to desk research, whether in libraries or on-line. Before visiting a library or logging-on, the information sought should be specified in some detail, although flexibility and some ingenuity are also needed (eg looking for relevant data under wider or narrower classifications and creatively making connections). Likely sources including 'sources of sources' can also be planned in advance, particularly as experience is gained. In the case of on-line database searching, a planned approach is particularly vital if log-on costs are to be kept to a minimum; the search strategy should be planned off- and not on-line.

The desk research plan should also include a timetable. How long should be spent on the desk research part of a project? This will depend on the breadth of the information sought, the type of data and the resources to be used. It is difficult to generalise. However, what can be said is that diminishing returns apply and after quite a short time, the extra information gained falls in proportion to the time spent searching.

Once found, data needs recording in the form of notes or photocopies. In the case of on-line searches the equivalent is down-loading into files. The source of any data should always be recorded, so that its accuracy can be both evaluated and, if necessary, retraced. Where reports quote such data the sources should be attributed. It is also good practice to keep working notes of all sources consulted or to be consulted whether or not these yield anything of value. In long projects and repeat work, this avoids the same blind alley being followed again.

Information needs not only collecting but evaluating. In part this is a matter of making judgements about its validity. Just because something is written down it is not necessarily true and the same applies to on-line databases. All secondary data accessed through desk research was originally generated through primary research and thorough validation requires going back to the source and understanding the methodology used – was it based on some sort of census, on a sample survey or merely on anecdotal evidence? Where possible two or more sources for the same data can be compared (although make sure they are different). However, some sense of proportion has to be kept. It is simply not possible to thoroughly validate in such ways all the data and nor is it necessary to do so – as previously mentioned (Chapter 2) accuracy levels can often be quite low for practical purposes.

As well as validating the data, evaluation also includes its integration into a meaningful whole. This is arguably an aspect of data analysis and reporting, the subject of Chapter 9. However, looking for linkages and patterns can and should be part of the desk research process with initial material often pointing to other sources and subjects. That is why we stated earlier that although planning is needed in desk research, flexibility should be retained. Subsequent analysis and integration of data will be facilitated by good note and record keeping when the material is collected and, if this is voluminous, by reasonably organised filing.

THE LIMITS OF DESK RESEARCH

Desk research can be very fruitful. However, it has its limits and it may only provide part of the information sought in a project. As previously suggested, where a mix of desk and primary research is likely to be required there is everything to be gained by carrying out desk research first and then filling the gaps through interviewing. In this way, the more expensive primary techniques are used only where essential.

One limit of desk research is its unpredictability. At least for the novice or where the subject area is unfamiliar, there can be no certainty of what the desk research will yield and what gaps will be left. This is partly the reason why desk research is not a major service of market research agencies; they find problems in offering and charging for an activity for which the client output is uncertain. However, the 'do your own' researcher need not be constrained in this way; at least a short desk research exercise will involve only modest costs and may save on much more expensive fieldwork. Unlike an agency, a 'do your own' researcher can live with little to show for the desk research stage.

Some information is also in principle not available from desk research and with a little experience this is obvious from the start. Generally this includes most attitude-type data, especially where the subject of consumer attitudes is particular rather than general – opinions of your own and competitor companies, of a novel product, of a specific advert, etc. However, even in research where the focus is attitudes and opinions, some background desk research may be useful – we have already given an example in relation to new product evaluation.

Between desk research and conventional fieldwork there are some useful hybrid activities which will be mentioned in the next chapter. These include simple observation as a means of data collection and 'overview' interviews, both techniques within the resources of any 'do your own' researcher.

List of sources

1. **British Library**, 96 Euston Road, St Pancras, London NW1 2DB. Tel: 0171 412 7677. Fax: 0171 412 7794.
2. **CSO Newport Library and Information Service**, Cardiff Road, Newport, Gwent NP9 1XG. Tel: 01633 812973.
3. **DTI Export Marketing Information Centre**, Ashdown House, 123 Victoria Street, London SW1E 5ED. Tel: 0171 215 5444.

4. **ASLIB**, The Association for Information Management, Staple Hall, Stone House Court, 87–90 Houndsditch, London EC3A 7PB. Tel: 0171 903 0000. Fax: 0171 903 0011.
5. **MAID/Profound**, The Communications Building, 48 Leicester Square, London WC2H 7DB. Tel: 0171 930 6900. Fax: 0171 930 6006.
6. **Dialog/Data-Star** (part of Dialog Corporation), 3rd Floor, Palace House, 3 Cathedral Street, London SE1 9DE. Tel: 0171 930 5503 and 0171 940 6900. Fax: 0171 940 6006.
7. **FT Profile**, Financial Times Information Ltd, Fitzroy House, 13–17 Epworth Street, London EC2A 4DL. Tel 0171 825 7902. Fax: 0171 825 7988.
8. *Annual Abstract of Statistics*, (previously HMSO) The Stationery Office Ltd, 49 High Holborn, London WC1V 6HB. Tel: 0171 873 0011.
9. *Guide to Official Statistics*, The Stationery Office (see ref 8).
10. **Eurostat**, Statistical Office of the European Communities, Jean Monnet Building, Rue Alcide de Gaspari, L-2920 Luxembourg. Tel: 00 35 2 4301-33454. Fax: 00 35 2 4301-32594.
11. **United Nations Information Centre**, 21st Floor, Millbank Tower, 21–24 Millbank, London SW1P 4QH. Tel: 0171 630 1981. Fax: 0171 976 6478.
12. **OECD**, 2 Rue André-Pascal, 75775 Paris CEDEX 16, France. Tel: 00 33 01.45.24.82.00. Fax: 00 33 01.45.24.85.00 (publications also from The Stationery Office – see ref 8).
13. **SMMT** – Society of Motor Manufacturers and Traders. Forbes House, Halkin Street, London SW1X 7DS. Tel: 0171 235 7000. Fax: 0171 235 7112.
14. *Directory of British Associations*, CBD Research, Chancery House, 15 Wickham Road, Beckenham, Kent BR3 5JS. Tel: 0181 650 7745. Fax: 0181 650 0768.
15 *Marketsearch*, Arlington Publications, 1 Hay Hill, Berkley Square, London W1X 7LF. Tel: 0171 495 1940.
16. *Findex*, available through Euromonitor, 60–61 Britton Street, London EC1M 5NA. Tel: 0171 251 1105. Fax: 0171 608 3149.
17. *The Financial Times*, Business Research Centre, 16–28 Tabernacle Street, London EC2A 4DD. Tel: 0171 970 0100.
18. **Research Index Ltd**, 94 West Parade, Lincoln LN1 1JZ. Tel: 01522 524212.
19. *BRAD*, Maclean Hunter Limited, Chalk Lane, Cockfosters Road, Barnet, Herts, EN4 0BU. Tel: 0181 242 3000. Fax: 0181 242 309820.

20. *Pims*, Pims UK Ltd, Midmay Avenue, London N1 4RS. Tel: 0171 226 1000.
21. *Kompass*, Reed Business Information, Windsor Court, East Grinstead, West Sussex RH19 1XA. Tel: 01342 326972.
22. *Key British Enterprises*, Dun & Bradstreet, Holmers Farm Way, High Wycombe, Bucks HP12 4UL. Tel: 01494 422000.
23. **Current British Directories**, CBD Research (see ref 14).
24. **Companies House**, Crown Way, Cardiff CF4 3UZ. Tel: 01222 388588.
25. **ICC Business Ratio Reports**, ICC, 72 Oldfield Road, Hampton, Middlesex TW12 2HQ. Tel: 0181 783 0922. www.keynote.co.uk.
26. **EXTEL**, EXTEL Financial Information Centre, 13 Epworth Street, London EC2A 4DL Tel: 0171 251 3333.
27. **Circare**, 108 Leonard Street, London EC2A 4RH. Tel: 0171 739 8424.
28. **Jordans**, 21 St Thomas Street, Bristol BS1 6JS. Tel: 0117 9230600.
29. *UK Markets*, Office of National Statistics, Cardiff Road, Newport, Mons. 1P9 1XG. Tel: 01633 815696.
30. *Market Assessment of Top Markets*, Market Assessment Publications, 5th Floor, 110 Strand, London WC2R 0AA. Tel: 0171 836 5111.
31. *Market Size Digest*, Mintel International Group, 18 Long Lane, London EC1A 9HE. Tel: 0171 606 4533.
32. *The UK Marketing Source Book*, NTC Publications, Farm Road, Henley on Thames, Oxfordshire RG9 1EJ. Tel: 01491 574671.
33. *The Source Book*, Keynote Publications, 72 Oldfield Road, Hampton, Middlesex TW12 2HQ. Tel: 0181 481 8760.
34. *The Guide*, Keynote Publications (see ref 33).
35. *European Directory of Marketing Information Sources*, Euromonitor (see ref 16).
36. *Directory of International Sources of Business Information* **(Ball)**, Pitman Publishers, 128 Long Acre, London WC2E 9AN. Tel: 0171 379 7383.
37. *On Line Business and Company Databases* **(Parkinson)**, ASLIB (see ref 4).
38. *Directory of On Line Databases*, Gale Research International, PO Box 699, North Way, Andover, Hants. SP10 1BE. Tel: 01264 342962.

4

Fieldwork

As discussed briefly at the end of Chapter 3, desk research, although a very important data collection technique, will not supply all information needs, and primary research through fieldwork may need to be used to fill the gaps. With few exceptions, market research fieldwork is based on sampling and the first part of this chapter discusses this topic both in theory and in practice. The various types of fieldwork are then discussed, although those most likely to be used in 'do your own' research are the subjects of separate and later chapters.

SAMPLING THEORY

Sampling is a major part of a market researcher's toolkit and although this book keeps theory to a minimum, a basic grasp of some of the fundamentals of sampling is needed to help avoid mistaken thinking and abuse of the data.

Information about a population, for example of the whole UK, can be collected by a census. The government carry out one every ten years and this provides vital data for market research. However, for most purposes a census is far too expensive to contemplate and unnecessary. The alternative is to collect the required data from a sample that represents the total population or group of interest (the universe). The brand awareness of a sample of consumers, for example, is taken to represent the awareness levels of all consumers. Similarly, the consumption of a product among a sample of companies is 'grossed up' to estimate total consumption levels or market size.

Confidence to use samples in this way is based on a branch of statistical theory which allows the accuracy levels of samples to be estimated within ranges of probabilities. Typically 95 per cent probability levels are taken and it might be said, for example, that if a measure taken in a sample (eg awareness levels of a brand) is 50 per cent, the accuracy level (or *sampling error*) at 95 per cent probability is ± 3 per cent. In other words we are confident that among the whole population there is a 95 per cent chance that the measure is between 47 per cent and 53 per cent (there is though a 5 per cent chance that the measure is outside these limits; complete certainty is not possible). The probability level – the chance of the sample measure being within the limits – does not have to be 95 per cent: it can be higher (eg 99 per cent) or lower (eg 90 per cent). At the lower probability the sampling error will be smaller (eg ± 1 per cent) but it is greater at the higher probability (eg ± 5 per cent). Note, however, that the sample is not any more or less accurate; it is just that the level of accuracy (sampling error) is expressed in different ways.

In estimating the accuracy of a sample, or selecting a sample to meet a required level of accuracy, there are two critical variables; the size of the sample and the measure being taken, which for simplicity we shall take as a single percentage, eg the percentage aware of a brand. A common mistake about sample size is to assume that accuracy is determined by the proportion of a population included in a sample (eg 10 per cent of a population). For most purposes this is not the case and what matters is the *absolute* size of the sample regardless of the size of population. A sample of 500 drawn from a population of 1 million will be as accurate as a sample of 500 from a population of 5 million. Figure 4.1 shows the link between sample size, sample measure and sampling error (ie accuracy), in this case at 95 per cent probability level.

In the figure the dotted line A intersects the 20 per cent sample measure on the left hand column and a sample size of 500 on the right hand column. The middle column shows the sampling error for this measure and sample size, about ± 3 per cent. Dotted line B passes through the same sample size of 500 but the measure in this case is 50 per cent and it will be seen that the sampling error is now about ± 4.5 per cent. The sampling error is in fact greatest for a 50 per cent measure*. The accuracy of a sample, therefore, depends on

---

*   With a simple either/or type of measure, a value of over 50 per cent has a corresponding converse value of less than 50 per cent (eg if 60 per cent are aware of an advert, logically, 40 per cent are not aware of it) and this value can be used in estimating sample accuracy (ie the sampling error for the 60 per cent measure is effectively the same as for 40 per cent).

the measure taken and to speak of a sample being accurate to say ±
5 per cent is strictly speaking misleading without reference to a
particular measure.

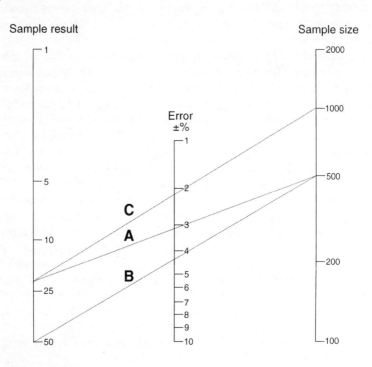

Figure 4.1 *Sampling error chart*

Line C on the chart shows the effect on accuracy levels of changing
the sample size. In this case the sample measure is also 20 per cent
(as line A) but the sample size is now 1000. The accuracy in this case
is shown to be about ± 2.25 per cent. An increase in accuracy level
has, therefore, been obtained by doubling the sample, but note that
this improvement is not proportional and a general rule is that the
gains in accuracy decline more than proportionately with increases
in sample size, a form of diminishing returns.

Figure 4.1 is not just for illustration and can be used to provide
a reasonable indication of sample accuracy, either to find the likely
accuracy range of a given sized sample or to find the sample needed
to achieve a given level of accuracy. In the examples discussed we
assumed that the sample measure had been found, but at the stage
at which sampling decisions are usually made this will not be the

case; the point of using a sample is to find the measure. In practice then it is usual to assume the 'worse case' measure of 50 per cent and select a sample on this basis. However, if the measure is expected to be well under 50%, the 'worst case' assumption would result in a sample size larger (and, therefore, more expensive) than is strictly needed.

An additional point about sample measures is that it is common to seek not only measures for the whole sample but for sub-samples within it. A sample of 500 adults drawn randomly, for example, is likely to include around 250 men and 250 women. Quite possibly it will be useful to look separately at the results from each sex – such differences (as well as for other demographics: age, income group, etc) may be vital in marketing planning. However, in looking separately at, say, men the effective sample is now 250 and the accuracy level is rather lower than for the whole sample of 500. This needs to be borne in mind when comparing differences between the data for men and women – a small difference may not be 'real' and simply reflect the sampling accuracy levels. Too many market research studies, including those carried out professionally, discuss differences between sub-samples where the numbers involved (bases) are just too small to allow inferences to be drawn with any reliability. The moral of this is that when planning samples it is important to think about which sub-groups may be important and to include sufficient numbers in each one.

The discussion of sampling (and sample accuracy) to this point assumes that the sample is *random,* ie that every member of the population being sampled has an equal chance of being included in the sample. Random samples are, however, difficult to achieve or even to closely approximate in practice. Selection from the electoral register, for example, may seem to be a form of rigorous random sampling of adults. However, the electoral register does not include all adults. For one reason or another a substantial proportion of the population is missed and therefore all adults do not have an equal chance of being included in any sample taken from this source (sampling frame). In other words any such sample is *biased* and the results from the sample cannot be assumed to be wholly representative of the whole population. Quite possibly those not on the register differ significantly from those who are included and it may well be that these differences are relevant to the purposes of the research being carried out.

A real example of such sampling bias, always mentioned, is a presidential election poll carried out in the USA in the 1930s. The poll was by phone and the results proved to be a quite inaccurate prediction of the election result. In this case the bias was against electors not on the phone (at a time when phone penetration was much lower than now), who differed in their voting intentions from richer citizens living in phone-connected households. In most surveys some such bias exists, although often the effects may not be serious enough to compromise the results. However, a researcher needs to be always on guard against such problems including where the samples are supplied from other sources, eg sales managers asked to select a sample of their customers may well have a bias towards customers who give them no problems.

Another problem area with even rigorously drawn random samples is non-response. For one reason or another it will in practice prove impossible to collect data from every individual making up a sample. Some will not be contactable, some may have moved away or died, and some will certainly refuse to participate. If the response rate achieved is 80 per cent then the *achieved sample* from the 500 originally selected will be only 400 and possibly the accuracy levels with this smaller sample will be too low. Of course the problem can be apparently solved by *sample replacement*: take a supplementary sample and make contact until the desired 500 interviews are achieved. However, we are back to problems of bias. The non-respondents may in some way or another differ significantly (in relation to the aims of the study) from those who were included in the sample and the results may not, therefore, be representative of the whole population.

In practical market research true random samples or even close approximations are seldom used. Either it is impractical to draw one (the cost of doing so might be too high) or for one reason or another it is not appropriate. For purposes of estimating sample accuracy levels, it is common practice to assume the sampling is random (ie apply statistical methods appropriate to random sampling), although strictly speaking this does not have a firm foundation. In consumer market research *quota sampling* is widely used as an alternative to random sampling. This involves selecting individuals for the sample to fill pre-set 'cells' so that the complete sample matches known characteristics of the population, eg social class and age. Table 4.1 illustrates this and in research using this sample respondents would be 'found' to match the characteristics of each cell (eg 12 respondents of social class C1 aged 18 to 24) until each cell is filled. Such samples are relatively cheap, compared to random or near random ones, but are much less rigorous and may entail unknown bias (introduced by how respondents are selected). Also problems of non-response still exist but usually cannot be quantified.

Table 4.1 *Example of interlocking quotas*

Age	Social Class				
	AB	C1	C2	DE	**Total**
18/24	2	12	8	11	33
25/44	12	19	18	16	65
45+	17	24	25	36	102
Total	31	55	51	63	**200**

Other approaches to consumer research sampling which come closer to random include *random walk,* where houses that are selected for contact are at predetermined intervals (eg every tenth) and along a pre-set route (eg first left, then right, etc). More expensive methods include *multi-stage sampling*, where areas (eg constituencies and wards) are selected randomly from listings and then contact households are chosen from the relevant electoral registers. Respondents may also be selected randomly from customer lists, although in this case various forms of potential bias may need to be thought through, eg dissatisfied customers who are no longer included in the list and recent customers who have not yet got on at all.

In business-to-business and industrial market research there are some special issues to consider of which the most important is that the sampling units, eg companies, are not of equal value as potential consumers. In research, for example, to establish the usage of a particular cable by telecommunications companies, a random selection from a complete listing of such companies may well not include BT (because it is only one out of, say, 500 listed). However, BT may account for 80 per cent of all the cable used and to miss the company would clearly produce results that could not be used to make estimates of the total market. A typical solution to this sort of problem is to set quotas – the same principle as in consumer market research but in this case based on company size – or to use *stratified sampling*; the listing of telecommunications companies is divided up into size bands, eg BT, other large, medium-sized and small companies, and samples then drawn from each strata. However, this assumes that the size of the companies can be established from secondary research. If this is not the case selection may be based on no more than informed judgement (possibly modified as interviews are carried out). Much business and industrial market research involves this sort of practical (if not theoretically robust) approach.

In Chapter 1 we drew a distinction between quantitative and qualitative research. The discussion of sampling so far has assumed that quantitative data is being sought. In qualitative research samples are also used but without much concern about accuracy levels. Typically only very small samples are used and the intention is in any case not to measure. It is common, however, in qualitative research to select samples on a quota basis so that they are 'representative' in a loose sort of sense. Problems of bias also need to be thought about; the results can be misleading if unintended bias excludes an important group from the research coverage.

PRACTICAL SAMPLING

With some basic theory out of the way we can now suggest how sampling can be practically planned. The starting point is the research objectives and coverage discussed in Chapter 2; this defines what information is being sought and the level of accuracy required and limitations to the research, for example geographical. Desk research may have already provided some of the information sought and sampling is a tool of the primary research required to fill in the gaps. There are three steps involved.

1. Define the population to be sampled.
2. Decide on the sample size and structure.
3. Choose a method of selecting the sample.

In our discussion of sampling theory we have not discussed the importance of defining the population to be sampled. Problems in research design often occur because insufficient thought is given to this. In consumer research the relevant population may be a 'natural' one, eg all adults in England. More often, however, it is a sub-group defined by some sort of behaviour, eg 'housewives', meaning those responsible for shopping for a household (and which in many households is now no longer either a wife or even a female) or consumers of a particular class of product (eg chocolate bars). This group certainly includes young children who determine brand choice even if they do not make the actual purchase). In business markets the population unit is usually companies or other sorts of organisations. Again these may be part of a defined industry or, quite often, consumers of some product or service. Establishing which type of company is involved may require an extensive screening exercise (eg initial contacts with a general sample of companies) or possibly may come out of the desk research. Another aspect of defining the population is deciding whether and which breakdowns of the total sample may be required. In consumer research this is often demographic groupings (eg age, sex, income group) and in business research, company size is often important. As already mentioned, the size of such sub-samples may be as important as the total sample size.

If the sample is to be used to produce quantitative data (estimates about the total population and possibly sub-groups) it must be large enough to be within the accuracy levels sought. The earlier part of this discussion covered the fundamentals of this, assuming a true random sample is used. Generally, sampling will not be random in the strict sense, but it is normal practice, if theoretically dubious, to assume that it is for the purposes of calculating sample accuracy and selecting an appropriate size. Figure 4.1 can, therefore, be used as a guide to an appropriate sample size, bearing in mind a possible need to have adequate sizes of sub-samples. Calculating an appropriate size of sample is not, therefore, a difficult task in theory. However, in practice, market researchers, and particularly those carrying out 'do your own' projects, commonly face the dilemma that the theoretically appropriate size of sample is way too large within the constraints of the available budget or for what can be practically carried out within a reasonable timescale. There is no way of fully squaring the circle. If the sample is smaller than that ideal optimum, the accuracy of the results will be compromised and at some point the accuracy levels may be so low that the research will simply not be accurate enough to guide, with any confidence, marketing decisions. And improving confidence in decision-making is what it is all supposed to be about. Sometimes, therefore, it is better to accept that within available resources, worthwhile research just cannot be done. However, often some compromise in accuracy levels can be accepted; as discussed earlier, accuracy is not an absolute virtue but depends on the purposes to which the data are to be put.

In any consumer research undertaken on a 'do your own' basis, quota sampling is likely to be the method used for sample selection. To prepare quotas, a profile of the population to be covered is required. Usually this can be obtained through desk research; there are several compendiums containing this sort of data including the modestly priced *Marketing Pocket Book**. One practical problem with quota sampling is that the numbers required within a sub-group (eg higher income groups) may be sufficient to meet the needs of the total sample size but too small to provide reliable results about a sub-group that may be of particular interest. The common solution to this problem is to 'over-sample' the sub-group (eg instead of say 10 per cent of the sample being in the upper income group this is increased to, say, 25 per cent) and have the results adjusted back to the true profile of the population at the data analysis stage through using weighting techniques (see Chapter 10).

In business research the sample is more commonly pre-selected from a listing of all companies within the industrial population being researched. In practice this often means from general or specialist directories. Sometimes no one directory or listing covers the whole population and several need to be combined (identifying which to use is part of the desk research stage). Whichever sources are used they should cover a high proportion of all companies in the industry and initial research may be needed to establish that this is the case. The work involved in abstracting and listing a sample from directories can be considerable but increasingly it is possible to access relevant databases on-line (eg from the *Kompass* directory publishers) and download the required sample. Costs will be incurred in doing this but these may well be less than that of clerical labour.

The last type of sample source to mention is customer lists. In customer satisfaction surveys and other types of studies the research population is a company's customers. To draw a reliable sample it is essential to start off with a complete listing of all customers and make a random or near random selection from this (eg taking every '*n*th' name from a random point where '*n*' is the interval needed to yield the required sample size). Where customer records are computerised it may be possible to do this work electronically. As previously mentioned, what must be avoided in customer sampling is any prior vetting of the list by the sales department to exclude troublesome customers. And a final point about customer sampling is that it can only yield customers. Quite possibly, to meet the research objectives, potential customers must also be considered and a sample of these will have to be drawn from another source.

---

*   Published by NTC (see source reference in Chapter 3).

FIELDWORK METHODS

Having decided on a sampling approach the next step in primary research design is to choose the fieldwork method. The main options are shown below.

- Observation techniques
     Retail distribution checks
     Retail audits
     Store traffic counts
     Mystery shopping
- Postal research
- Phone interviews
- Face-to-face interviews
- Venue based research (eg hall tests)
- Qualitative fieldwork
     Group discussions
     Depth interviews
- Overview interviews

Postal research, phone interviews and face-to-face interviews are generally regarded as the main fieldwork methods and each is the subject of a separate chapter (6, 7 and 8). In the remainder of this chapter we discuss some of the other techniques.

Fieldwork is often equated with interviewing but this is not necessarily the case; there are two important methods that do not involve an interviewer or equivalent questioning of a respondent: postal research (which is discussed in Chapter 6) and observation. Observation techniques cover a variety of approaches, some specialised and not practical for 'do your own' research, but others can be both simple to carry out and very useful. In research concerned with retail distribution for example, a check of brands or product lines in stock in particular types of retail outlet can yield important data. This work may be carried out with limited resources if the sample of outlets is kept small, requires little skill or training and does not normally need the permission or cooperation of the shop management. In this case the sampling population is all retail outlets of the type to be included and the principles of sample selection, previously discussed, need to be considered, including stratifying by large, medium and small outlets. The more sophisticated version of this type of observation is full blown retail audits involving measuring the sales of goods through outlets. The concept is not difficult. Prior to bar scanning tills (which now provide point of sale data), measurement involved stock level counts at the start and end of the period and establishing deliveries in between, but the organisation of this type of research is a formidable task, requiring involvement of and payment to retail outlets and is the province of a few specialised research companies (eg AGB Taylor Nelson and Nielsen). Retail auditing is not within the practical scope of 'do your own' research unless the outlets are in some sense tame or tied.

Another possible retail measure is store traffic counts – the number of customers entering or leaving an outlet. By sampling over a representative period (which obviously must include weekends) estimates can be made of total traffic at an outlet. The technique can also be extended to other sorts of visitor counts, for example to a park. Again little skill or training is needed for the work, just a certain endurance.

A type of observation-based research which has become increasingly used is so-called *mystery shopping*. The sort of data sought here is the quality and perhaps uniformity of service by such as shop staff – important aspects of customer satisfaction research. This technique can provide a more direct measure of service levels than asking customers to recall their experiences after the event. The technique involves researchers posing as customers and experiencing the service provided. If the goods or service involved are of trivial cost, an actual purchase may be made but otherwise the 'customer' may back-off just before the point of commitment (eg after receiving an insurance quotation). The practical limitation of the technique is that the 'shopper' must be convincing. This is not hard in the case of most domestic products or services but very much more difficult in business markets – for example real fleet operators do not drop into truck dealers to buy a 40 tonne vehicle. There are also some ethical issues (and possibly even legal ones) to consider when store staff's time is wasted by mystery shoppers and where the feedback may adversely affect individual staff. Much depends on how much time is wasted and how the data are reported and used. However, with these reservations, mystery shopping can be a practical technique for 'do your own' research. Again sampling principles apply.

With ingenuity, other variants on observation can also be considered for research projects including to estimate the population of objects rather than people – eg construction methods used in various types of building – and how equipment and materials are actually used. The authors, for example, in researching a new pack for electric cable, observed how electricians actually handled cable reels.

As already mentioned, the main interviewing techniques are discussed in separate chapters and nothing needs adding here. There are, however, some specialised variants that at least ought to be mentioned even though they are, in the main, not realistic options for 'do your own' projects.

Research projects may require consumer reactions to a product, for example to establish potential acceptance of a new product. Often this involves 'blind' testing (with the brand obscured) and comparisons against other products. There are two approaches: *hall tests* and *home placements*. Hall tests (sometimes called clinics) involve recruiting a sample of respondents to come into a venue (the hall) where they are exposed to the products in a controlled way and then interviewed. In a particular project, the test may be repeated in several locations with possibly 100 or more respondents covered in each. Home placement, as the name suggests, involves leaving products with a sample of consumers and following-up with a face-to-face or phone interview. The nature of the product (eg an intimate one) may favour this method over hall tests, although the research usually takes longer to complete and the exposure of the product is less controlled. Both hall tests and home placement require staffing levels that are usually beyond the resources of a 'do your own' researcher. Also, if food products are concerned, skill, knowledge and possibly qualifications are needed to ensure safe handling; the various regulatory bodies take an increasing interest in this area.

Qualitative research (see Chapter 1) involves distinct methods, mainly *depth interviews* and *group discussions* (termed focus groups in the USA). Depth interviews are really variants of face-to-face interviews, discussed in Chapter 8. They are generally minimally structured and require skill, training and experience. The 'do your own' researcher can in time become competent in this type of research; serving some type of apprenticeship with an experienced researcher is by far the best way of acquiring the skills. With no attempt at quantification in this type of work, small samples are usually involved. This makes the technique a practical undertaking for one researcher working alone.

Group discussions also involve skill and experience, but in this case it is the logistics of setting up a group that is usually beyond the scope of 'do your own' research. Group recruitment can, however, be bought-in as a separate service – see Chapter 10. The 'group' is around eight respondents, selected to some qualifying criteria (eg demographics or product usage) who meet together, in an informal venue, to discuss a subject of interest to the researcher, eg attitudes to brand names. The discussion, lasting one or more hours, is led by the researcher – the 'moderator' – and skill is needed to manage the group and facilitate their interaction to reveal and articulate beliefs and attitudes. Visual prompts of various sorts may be used to stimulate the discussion. Normally several separate groups are held and the resulting tape recordings analysed and integrated, itself a painstaking task. An important practical aspect of group discussion research is that the meeting is only the tip of the iceberg. As well as the analysis time afterwards, recruitment of suitable respondents and persuading them to turn up on time for the discussion (a small incentive is given) is a major task and typically takes several days per group. This is why group discussion research, quite apart from the skills required*, is probably not a practical undertaking in 'do your own' projects.

The last specialised form of fieldwork to mention is *overview interviews*. These may be carried out face-to-face or by phone. The techniques discussed in Chapters 7 and 8 largely apply. What distinguishes these sorts of interview is that they are not carried out with a sample of consumers but with a few selected experts who give an opinion or knowledge about a whole market or sector rather than just of their own (or organisation's) behaviour or attitudes. Relevant respondents may be journalists (eg from trade journals), officers of trade associations, technical experts or leading suppliers to an industry – whoever may have the knowledge which is sought. The interview itself is a discussion rather than a structured question-and-answer session, although some form of topic checklist is essential. Often, both respondents and subjects arise from initial desk research. This sort of fieldwork is well within the resources of a 'do your own' researcher and may often be a more efficient and practical source of data than end-user interviews (in industrial markets, overview interviews may be the only practical means of estimating market size, etc). The main skill is gaining cooperation, and the principles discussed in later chapters apply. Some respondents may reasonably ask for payment in return for their expert

---

*   One method of building these skills is to sit in on groups led by experienced researchers. It is common practice for clients to attend groups commissioned from professional research specialists.

knowledge. Where the overview respondent is in some sense a competitor a particularly sensitive approach is needed – often based on an exchange of information so that the respondent also gains. Ethical considerations should apply and respondents must not be mislead about the purpose of the interview.

Whatever form of fieldwork is used, a questionnaire or similar tool (eg discussion checklists, observation sheets) is essential. Designing effective questionnaires is the subject of Chapter 5.

5

Questionnaires

A questionnaire is a structured sequence of questions designed to draw out facts and opinions from respondents and provide a vehicle for recording the data. This chapter begins with a discussion of the role of questionnaires and presents a fully formatted example with a variety of question layouts. A description of the different types of questions and questionnaires follows. Finally, we recommend procedures for designing a questionnaire and show the pitfalls to avoid.

THE FOUR PURPOSES OF QUESTIONNAIRES

Questionnaires fulfil four purposes. Their first and prime role is to draw accurate information from respondents. Whilst drafting a questionnaire, the researcher is forced to give detailed consideration to the information required to meet the project objectives. This ensures that the right questions are asked.

Secondly, questionnaires provide structure to interviews. In any survey of more than a very small sample, it is important that all respondents are asked the same questions in the same way. Without this structure it would be impossible to build an overall picture. Questionnaires make the interviewers' task easier as they coordinate all the people working on the survey, instructing them exactly what to say and when. For respondents they smooth the interview process as the orderly sequence of questions drives logically towards a point.

The third purpose of questionnaires is to provide a standard form on which facts, comments and attitudes can be written down. A record of an interview is essential, as without it points would be forgotten or distorted. Paper questionnaires are the simplest template for capturing data. In large studies market research agencies are making increasing use of computers for this purpose. In studies of a couple of dozen interviews, a tape recorder could be used as well as or instead of a questionnaire. However, tape recorders can run out, break down, and sometimes they inhibit respondents. Also the tapes are time consuming to transcribe and interpret. Besides, even when a tape is used, a questionnaire (or at the very least a list of questions) is also needed to guide the discussion.

Fourthly and finally, questionnaires facilitate data processing. Answers are recorded in a common place on each questionnaire so that simple counts can be made of how many people said what. Without a questionnaire, a survey of 500 people would produce 500 jottings or free-ranging interviews, which would be impossible to process.

At this early stage it may be helpful for the reader to view a questionnaire in its entirety. Some of the principles embodied in its design will become apparent from our comments. The questionnaire provided as an example was administered by telephone and the interview took between 15 and 20 minutes to complete.

TYPES OF QUESTIONNAIRE

There are three different types of interview situation which in turn require different types of questionnaire.

- *Structured.* In structured interviews, the questionnaires set out the precise wording of the questions and the order in which they are asked. Most of the questions have pre-coded responses and there is little latitude to stray beyond them. Structured questionnaires and interviews are used in large, quantitative surveys.
- *Semi-structured.* This type of interview employs questions with pre-coded responses as well as those where respondents' comments are written down verbatim. The semi-structured questionnaire is a flexible tool allowing probing to find out the reasons for certain answers. However, it is expensive to analyse the open-ended questions and therefore tends to be used in samples of 200 or less.
- *Unstructured.* In unstructured interviews the researcher uses a checklist of questions, capturing the responses as notes or on tape. The interviewer is allowed considerable latitude and will draft questions as appropriate, exploring avenues raised in the discussion and not necessarily covered on the checklist. Generally only a couple of dozen interviews of this kind are carried out in a survey as each response script is unique in some way and it is difficult to pull them all together.

ALUMINIUM WINDOW SURVEY

Company Name: . . . .

Address: . . . .

. . . .

. . . .

Respondent Name & Position: . . . .

Fieldworker: . . . .

Date: . . . .

Good morning/afternoon. This is . . . . . from Business & Market Research in Manchester. I am carrying out a survey into trends in the aluminium window market and I wonder if you could help me. It will only take about fifteen minutes. Before I start can I make sure that you fabricate domestic aluminium windows or doors? (ONLY INTERVIEW COMPANIES THAT DO SO).

Q1.   First of all, can I check if you fabricate any other types of domestic replacement windows or doors?

UPVC	1
Softwood	2
Hardwood	3
Steel	4
Only aluminium	5
Others (SPECIFY)	6

. . . .

Roughly, what proportion of your domestic window or door business, in value terms is in . . . . . . (SPECIFY THE DIFFERENT MATERIALS FROM WHICH THE FABRICATORS MAKES WINDOWS)?

		<5%	6-20%	21-40%	41-60%	61-85%	86-99%	100%	None
Q2a	Aluminium?	1	2	3	4	5	6	7	8
Q2b	UPVC?	1	2	3	4	5	6	7	8
Q2c	Softwood?	1	2	3	4	5	6	7	8
Q2d	Hardwood?	1	2	3	4	5	6	7	8
Q2e	Steel?	1	2	3	4	5	6	7	8
Q2f	Other?	1	2	3	4	5	6	7	8

Q3a. What particular advantages does a domestic aluminium range offer you? (DO NOT PROMPT)

Meets customer demand	1
Offers an alternative	2
Looks better in certain houses	3
Stronger/more durable	4
Easier to fabricate	5
Cheaper/better value than UPVC	6
Wider range of finish/colours	7
Low maintenance	8
Good insulation properties	9
Condensation free	10
Other (SPECIFY)	11
....	12

(ASK ONLY IF UPVC WINDOWS ARE FABRICATED)

Q3b. What particular advantages does a UPVC domestic range offer you?
(DO NOT PROMPT)

Meets customer demand	1
Offers an alternative	2
Looks better in certain houses	3
Stronger/more durable	4
Easier to fabricate	5
Cheaper/better value than UPVC	6
Wider range of finish/colours	7
Low maintenance	8
Good insulation properties	9
Condensation free	10
Other (SPECIFY)	11
....	12

Q4a. Looking to the future, would you expect your sales of aluminium windows or doors for the domestic market, to increase, decrease or stay the same over the next three years?

Increase	1	Q4b
Stay the same/don't know	2	Q4d
Decrease	3	Q4d
Refused	4	Q4f

Q4b. Why do you think that your sales of domestic aluminium windows will increase over the next three years? (DO NOT PROMPT)

Market buoyant/increasing	1
Innovations in aluminium design	2
Aluminium more competitive	3
UPVC degenerates over time	4
Aluminium easier to work with	5
Aluminium more profitable for me	6
Will push aluminium more in future	7
Other (SPECIFY)	8
....	9

Q4c. Can I ask you to imagine that your sales of domestic aluminium windows and doors are 100 at the present, what do you think they could be in three years time, in 1996?

100	1
101 - 105	2
106 - 110	3
111 - 120	4
121 - 140	5
141 - 150	6
151 - 180	7
Over 180	8
Don't know	9

Q4d. Why do you think that your sales of aluminium windows and doors will stay the same/decline over the next three years?

UPVC will steal sales	1
Hardwood will steal sales	2
Competition fierce in aluminium	3
Fall in demand for replacement windows	4
Not a profitable market	5
Will get out of aluminium in future	6
Other (SPECIFY)	7
....	8

Q4e. Can I ask you to imagine that your sales of domestic aluminium windows or doors are 100 at the present, what do you think they could be in three years time in 1996?

100	1
90 - 99	2
80 - 89	3
60 - 79	4
50 - 59	5
Will get out of aluminium by then	6
Don't know	7

ASK ALL

Q4f. What changes do you foresee within the market for different types of domestic aluminium systems? PROBE: What about thermal brakes? What about different colours? What about finishes? What about doors as opposed to windows - which do you think will grow faster?

....

....

Q5a. Could I now ask you which manufacturers you are aware of that supply domestic aluminium systems to companies such as yourself? PROBE: Any others? DO NOT PROMPT.

Q5b. I am now going to read out some other companies that supply this market. As I read them out, would you tell me which you have heard of? **READ OUT ONLY THOSE NOT RINGED AT Q5a. ROTATE THE ORDER PLEASE.**

	Q5a	Q5b
Adeptal	1	1
Alcan	2	2
AWS	3	3
Cego Crittall	4	4
Coastal	5	5
Consort	6	6
Duraflex	7	7
Glostal	8	8
HIS	9	9
Monarch	10	10
Prime	11	11
Scope	12	12
Schuco	13	13
Smart Systems	14	14
Other (SPECIFY)	15	15
....	16	16

Now could I check out your views on some of these system companies that you are aware of. Which do you think is best in the domestic aluminium market for. . .?

Q6a. delivery?

Q6b. price?

Q6c. quality?

	Q6a	Q6b	Q6c
Adeptal	1	1	1
Alcan	2	2	2
AWS	3	3	3
Cego Crittall	4	4	4
Coastal	5	5	5
Consort	6	6	6
Duraflex	7	7	7
Glostal	8	8	8
HIS	9	9	9
Monarch	10	10	10
Prime	11	11	11
Scope	12	12	12
Schuco	13	13	13
Smart Systems	14	14	14
Other (SPECIFY)	15	15	15
....	16	16	16

Q7a. And now finally in this series of questions on companies, can I ask you which companies you use yourselves as suppliers of domestic aluminium systems?

Adeptal	1
Alcan	2
AWS	3
Cego Crittall	4
Coastal	5
Consort	6
Duraflex	7
Glostal	8
HIS	9
Monarch	10
Prime	11
Scope	12
Schuco	13
Smart Systems	14
Other (SPECIFY)	15
....	16

Q7b. Are there any other companies supplying domestic aluminium systems that you would not use?

Yes	1	**Q7c**
No	2	**Q8a**

Q7c. Which companies are they?

Adeptal	1
Alcan	2
AWS	3
Cego Crittall	4
Coastal	5
Consort	6
Duraflex	7
Glostal	8
HIS	9
Monarch	10
Prime	11
Scope	12
Schuco	13
Smart Systems	14
Other (SPECIFY)	15
....	16

Q7d. Why wouldn't you use this company? (STATE COMPANY IF RESPONDENT WOULDN'T USE MORE THAN ONE)?

....

....

Q8a. What above all else do you look for when choosing an aluminium system supplier for domestic window or door frames? **PROMPT & ROTATE FACTORS.**

Wide range of aluminium systems	1
Rapid delivery	2
Assured delivery	3
Competitive prices	4
Technical advice	5
Good sales service	6
High quality systems	7
(Don't know)	8

Q8b. Is there anything else important?

Yes	1	**Q8c**
No	2	**Q9a**

Q8c. What else is important?

....

....

Q9a. I am on the last leg now and you have been most patient. My final questions are simply to classify the information you have just given me. As with all the data it will be treated as absolutely confidential to ourselves. Which of the following activities are you involved in for the domestic market? **READ OUT LIST**

Aluminium windows	1
Aluminium doors	2
UPVC windows	3
UPVC doors	4
Other windows	5
Other doors	6
(Refused)	7

Q9b. Are there any other important sides to your business outside of these I have just mentioned?

Yes	1	**Q9c**
No	2	**Q10a**

Q9c. What else do you do?

....

....

Very roughly, what proportion of your business in aluminium windows and doors is....

		<5%	5-30%	31-80%	81-99%	100%	DK/not stated	None
Q10a	domestic?	1	2	3	4	5	6	7
Q10b	commercial or industrial?	1	2	3	4	5	6	7

Q11.   What were your total purchases of aluminium section used for domestic replacement windows and doors in 1993? Please exclude any section that may be used to reinforce UPVC windows or doors. RECORD ANSWER IN EITHER £ OR TONNES BELOW.

Under £25k (33 tonnes)	1
£26k - £200k (34 - 267 tonnes)	2
£201k - £750k (268 - 1,000 tonnes)	3
£751k - £1,500k (1,001 - 2,000 tonnes)	4
£1,501 - £2,500 (2,001 - 3,333 tonnes)	5
Over £2,500k (3,334 + tonnes)	6
Don't know/won't say/refused	7

Q12.   LOCATION

North	1
Midlands	2
South	3

THANK & CLOSE

The three classifications of questionnaires are summarised below.

TYPE OF QUESTIONNAIRE	AREAS OF USE OF QUESTIONNAIRE	ADMINISTRATION OF THE QUESTIONNAIRE
Structured	Used in large interview programmes (anything over 50 interviews). Typically where it is possible to closely anticipate the responses.	Telephone/ face-to-face self-completion.
Semi-structured	Used widely in business-to-business market research where there is a need to accommodate widely different responses from companies. Also used where the responses can not be anticipated.	Face-to-face/ telephone.
Unstructured	The basis of many studies into technical or narrow markets. Used in depth interviewing and group discussions. Allows probing and searching where the researcher is not fully sure of the responses before the interview.	Group discussions/ face-to-face interviews/depth telephone interviews.

TYPES OF QUESTION

Structured and semi-structured questionnaires are made up of three different types of questions depending on the information that is being collected.

TYPE OF QUESTION	INFORMATION SOUGHT	TYPES OF SURVEYS WHERE USED
Behavioural	Factual information on what the respondent is, does or owns. Also the frequency with which certain actions are carried out. Where people live.	Surveys to find out market size, market shares, awareness and usage.
Attitudinal	What people think of something. Their image and ratings of things. Why they do things.	Image and attitude surveys. Brand mapping studies. Customer satisfaction surveys.
Classification	Information that can be used to group respondents to see how they differ one from the other – such as their age, gender, social class, location of household, type of house, family composition.	All surveys.

Behavioural questions

Behavioural questions are designed to find out what people (or companies) do. For example, do people go to the cinema? How often do they go? What type of films do they watch? Who do they go with? They determine people's actions in terms of what they have eaten (or drunk), bought, used, visited, seen, read or heard. Behavioural questions record *facts* and not matters of opinion.

Common forms of behavioural question

- Have you ever...?
- Do you ever...?
- Who do you know...?
- When did you last...?
- Which do you do most often...?
- Who does it...?
- How many...?

- Do you have...?
- In what way do you do it...?
- In the future will you...?

Attitudinal questions

People hold opinions or beliefs on everything from politics to social precepts, to the products they buy and the companies which make or supply them. These attitudes are not necessarily right, but this is hardly relevant since it is *perceptions* which count. People's attitudes guide the way they act.

Common forms of attitudinal question

- Why do you...?
- What do you think of...?
- Do you agree or disagree...?
- How do you rate...?
- Which is best (or worst) for...?

Whereas answers to behavioural questions can be assumed to be correct (unless someone is deliberately lying or the question is stretching the bounds of their ability to answer), determining the level of people's beliefs and attitudes is not always clear cut. Researchers try to gauge attitudes to precepts, products, services or suppliers using *scales* a most common one having five points and ranging from very likely through to very unlikely, ie:

- Very likely
- Quite likely
- Neither likely nor unlikely
- Quite unlikely
- Very unlikely

Attitudes can also be measured by reading out (or showing cards) statements and asking respondents to what extent they agree or disagree with them. A mixture of positive and negative statements in the listing makes sure that the respondents do not get into a rut of agreeing (or disagreeing) with each question.

Classification questions

The third group of questions are those used to *classify* the information once it has been collected. Classification questions check that the correct quota of people or companies have been interviewed and are used to make comparisons between different groups of respondents. Most classification questions are behavioural (factual).

Typical classification questions are used to build a profile of respondents by finding out their age, their sex, their social class, where they live, their marital status, the type of house they live in, the number of people in their family, etc.

A number of standard classification questions crop up constantly in consumer market research surveys. These are as follows.

Sex

There can be no classifications other than male and female.

Household status

Traditionally, most researchers classify adults into three groups:

Head of household	☐
Housewife	☐
Other adult	☐

However, demographic and lifestyle changes are making this breakdown of doubtful value.

Marital status

This is usually asked by simply saying 'Are you...'

Single	☐
Married	☐
Widowed	☐
Divorced	☐
Separated	☐

Socio-economic grade

This is a classification used by UK market researchers in which respondents are pigeonholed according to the occupation of the head of the household. Thus, it combines the attributes of income, education and work status. In addition to social grades, researchers sometimes classify respondents by income group or lifestyle.

In summary the socio-economic grades are:

A   higher managerial, administrative or professional
B   intermediate managerial, administrative or professional

C1   Supervisory, clerical, junior administrative or professional
C2   skilled manual workers
D   semi-skilled and unskilled manual workers
E   state pensioners, widows, casual and lowest grade workers.

For most practical purposes these can be reduced to just four:

AB   □
C1   □
C2   □
DE   □

Working status

In surveys of the general public, it may be relevant to establish the level of employment of the respondent. For example:

Working full time (over 30 hours a week)	□
Working part-time (8–30 hours a week)	□
Housewife (full time at home)	□
Student (full time)	□
Retired	□
Temporarily unemployed (but seeking work)	□
Permanently unemployed (eg chronically sick, independent means, etc)	□

Location

Depending on the scope of the survey, this can be according to one of the Standard Regions of the UK, ITV reception areas or even a simple split into North, Midlands and South.

Neighbourhood

People can be classified according to the type of neighbourhood in which they live. These are often referred to as ACORN or PINPOINT classifications after the market research companies which devised them. They group people into neighbourhood types such as:

Agricultural areas	□
Modern family houses, higher incomes	□
Older houses of intermediate status	□
Poor quality older terraced housing	□
Better off council estates	□

Less well off council estates ☐
Poorest council estates ☐
Multi-racial areas ☐
High status, non-family areas ☐
Affluent suburban housing ☐
Better off retirement areas ☐
Unclassified ☐

Classification questions for industrial or business-to-business research commonly include industry and size of firm.

Industry

Researchers often condense the many divisions of the Standard Industrial Classification (referred to usually as SIC) into more convenient and broader groupings. These could be as simple as:

Primary (farming, forestry, fishing, quarrying, etc) ☐
Manufacturing ☐
Retailing and distribution ☐
Service industries ☐
Public service ☐
Armed forces ☐
Education ☐
Professions (doctors, dentists, architects, etc) ☐

Size of firm

The size of the firm in which the respondent works can be classified according to the number of employees:

0 – 9 ☐
10 – 24 ☐
25 – 99 ☐
100 – 249 ☐
250+ ☐

Open ended or closed questions and scales

Behavioural, attitudinal or classification questions can be open ended or closed. Scales are a special type of closed question.

Open ended questions, as the name suggests, leave the respondent free to give any answer. Although the question may be asked in open ended fashion, the researcher may have given thought to the possible answers and have listed a number of alternatives on the questionnaire. The respondent would be unaware of these and they are there for the greater efficiency of completing the questionnaire and the subsequent data processing. Such a question is open ended but has some pre-coded responses.

The second style of question is a closed or prompted question. Here the replies have been anticipated, are read out or are shown on a card and respondents are asked to choose whichever best indicates their answer. The pre-defined answers are worked out by common sense, as a result of earlier qualitative research or through a pilot study.

The third style of question is a scale – a special type of closed question. Scales could use either words (eg see page 63), numbers or even diagrams to measure people's attitudes and behaviour.

PRINCIPLES OF QUESTIONNAIRE DESIGN

If questionnaires fail it is usually because they are dashed off with insufficient thought. Questions are missed out, badly constructed, too long, complicated and sometimes unintelligible. Questionnaire design is a refining process in which a rough draft is eventually converted to a precise and formatted document. It would be unusual (and dangerous) to design a questionnaire without at least three edits. Here are ten rules to think about when designing a questionnaire.

1. *Think about the objectives of the survey.* As discussed in Chapter 2, the research plan for a project should include a statement of the overall objectives and an outline of the required information coverage. Looking back to this plan will ensure that all the required information is covered in the questionnaire; the information coverage is virtually a topic list from which specific questions can be developed. Obviously, any of the overall coverage which has been met through desk research can be omitted from the scope of the questionnaire.
2. *Think about how the interview will be carried out.* The way that the interview will be carried out will have a bearing on the framing of the questions. For example, open-ended questions usually result in poor replies in self-completion questionnaires. See also comments on the style of question appropriate to the main interviewing methods in Chapters 6, 7 and 8.
3. *Think about the 'boiler plate' information.* Every questionnaire

needs 'boiler plate' or standard information such as the name and address of the respondent, the date of the interview and the name of the interviewer.

4. *Think about the visual appearance.* The questionnaire should make effective use of white space so that it is clear and easy to read. Questions and response options should be laid out in a standard format and the typeface should be large enough to read (bearing in mind the likely interviewing conditions). Where appropriate, there should be ample space to write in open-ended comments.

5. *Think about the introduction.* People are more inclined to co-operate with researchers if they consider the survey to be bona fide and have a legitimate purpose. The introduction should explain why the survey is being carried out and provide an assurance of confidentiality.

6. *Think about the order of the questions.* The questions should flow easily from one to another and be grouped into topics in a logical sequence.

7. *Think about the types of questions.* Texture in the interview can be achieved by incorporating different styles of questions. The researcher can choose from open-ended questions, closed questions and scales.

8. *Think about the possible answers at the same time as thinking about the questions.* The whole purpose of questions is to derive answers and so it is essential that some thought is given to these, since they may, in turn, influence the shape of the question. For example, it is no good asking wholesalers how many they sell each year if their time horizon is a week or a month.

9. *Think about how the data will be processed.* A coding system should be used which suits the way in which it will be analysed, for example, on a spreadsheet or using proprietary market research software. In a survey involving over 30 respondents, analysing the free-ranging (open-ended) responses is laborious and thought should be given to using pre-coded responses wherever this is practical.

10. *Think about interviewer instructions.* Where questionnaires are administered by someone other than their designer, the interviewer (or the respondent in the case of self-completion questionnaires) needs clear guidance on what to do at each point in the questionnaire. These instructions need to be differentiated from the text either by capital letters or by emboldened or underlined type.

There are also a number of pitfalls to avoid in questionnaire design. These are some tips on what to do and not to do when designing questionnaires.

- *Ensure that questions are without bias.* Questions should not be worded in such a way as to lead the respondent into the answer.
- *Make the questions as simple as possible.* Questions should not only be short, they should also be simple. Those which include multiple ideas or two questions in one will confuse and be misunderstood.
- *Make the questions very specific.* Notwithstanding the importance of brevity and simplicity, there are occasions when it is advisable to lengthen the question by adding memory cues. For example, it is good practice to be specific with time periods.
- *Avoid jargon or shorthand.* It cannot be assumed that respondents will understand words commonly used by researchers. Trade jargon, acronyms and initials should be avoided unless they are in everyday use.
- *Steer clear of sophisticated or uncommon words.* A questionnaire is not a place to score literary points so only use words in common parlance. Colloquialisms are acceptable if they will be understood by everybody (some are highly regional).
- *Avoid ambiguous words.* Words such as 'usually' or 'frequently' have no specific meaning and need qualifying.
- *Avoid questions with a negative in them.* Questions are more difficult to understand if they are asked in a negative sense. It is better to say 'Do you ever...?', as opposed to 'Do you never ...?'
- *Avoid hypothetical questions.* It is difficult to answer questions on imaginary situations. Answers may be given but they cannot necessarily be trusted.
- *Do not use words which could be misheard.* This is especially important when the interview is administered over the telephone. On the telephone, 'what is your opinion of sects?' could yield interesting but not necessarily relevant answers.
- *Desensitise questions by using response bands.* Questions which ask respondents' age or companies' turnover are often best in the form of a pre-coded range of response bands. This softens the question by indicating that a broad answer is acceptable. Since such data will almost certainly be grouped into bands at the analysis stage, it may as well be collected in this way. However, not all numerical measures should be obtained like this since sometimes the researcher may have no real idea of the intervals

into which the responses will fall (see also comments in Chapter 9).

- *Ensure that fixed responses do not overlap*. The categories which are used in a fixed response question should be sequential and mutually exclusive, for example over 18 to 25, over 25 to 30, etc and not 18/25, 25/30 (where does 25 fall?).
- *Allow for 'others' in fixed response questions*. Pre-coded answers should always allow for a response other than those listed. It should be noted that these 'other' responses will always be under-recorded.

GETTING THE QUESTIONNAIRE TO WORK

Before starting interviewing or giving the questionnaire to an interviewing team, the researcher should at the very least read it out aloud. Better still, ask a colleague to play the role of respondent. Using the spoken word exposes weaknesses in wording or phraseology and highlights inconsistencies.

Ideally the questionnaire should then be *piloted*: interviewing a small number of respondents and reviewing the questionnaire before going ahead with the main stage of the fieldwork. In many surveys, half a dozen to 20 interviews will be sufficient to establish if the questionnaire really does work.

6

Postal Research and Self-completion Questionnaires

A 'do your own' researcher can carry out a sizeable study with comparative ease by means of a postal survey. Once the physical task of printing and mailing the questionnaires is complete, the researcher can sit back as the fieldwork takes care of itself. (Actually, it is not quite as relaxing as we imply since there is always uncertainty about response rates.)

In this chapter we show when to use postal surveys and how to obtain the best response rates. The importance of the cover letter is discussed and a sample is provided. Finally, we look at the costs of postal research compared to other methods of interviewing and provide advice on planning a postal survey.

WHEN POSTAL AND SELF-COMPLETION RESEARCH IS APPROPRIATE

The choice of research method in any survey is influenced by the type of information required, the nature of respondents, the budget and the timetable. Postal surveys work best where there is a high quality mailing list and respondents can easily be identified. They are eminently suitable when the information required is relatively simple, respondents are committed or feel obliged to reply and when respondents can be identified by name so that the questionnaires can be personally addressed.

Where lists are deficient or the information that is sought is qualitative, unstructured, detailed or complicated in some way, then self-completion questionnaires are not recommended. Nor are self-completion questionnaires appropriate in circumstances where respondents lack the motivation to fill them in.

In this chapter we are principally concerned with postal surveys as these are useful to the 'do your own' researcher. This said, self-completion questionnaires can be used in face-to-face interviews in the right circumstances, often for scalar questions where it is easier for respondents to read the questions and tick the boxes themselves rather than go through the rigmarole of having the interviewer read everything out. Many of the principles of postal questionnaires are the same as for self-completion questions used during a face-to-face interview. Self-completion questionnaires can now also be considered over the Internet and this may become a significant method in the future. Of course all the problems of non-response bias, discussed in Chapter 4, still apply.

FACTORS AFFECTING THE RESPONSE RATE IN POSTAL SURVEYS

Researchers are understandably nervous about losing control in surveys, especially if this could result in a poor response rate. When response rates fall much below 50 per cent of the attempted sample, there is a danger that the results will be in some way atypical. Only in exceptional conditions can response rates of over 50 per cent be achieved from postal surveys and more normally they are around 25–35 per cent. This need not mean that the results are unreliable, it simply means that it is not possible to state how reliable they really are. If the subject does not suit postal research, response rates could fall below 10 per cent, in which case the results could be highly suspect.

A number of factors influence the response rates.

Interest in the subject

The factor that influences the response rate of a postal survey more than anything else is the interest that respondents have in the subject. A postal survey of customers is likely to achieve a higher response than one of non-customers because there is an interest in and a relationship between customers and the sponsor of the study. So too, a postal survey aimed at transport managers in companies which have just bought a new truck will generate a high response (over 30 per cent and possibly over 50 per cent) because they are interested in the vehicle. People who have recently bought a new car frequently receive a postal questionnaire of considerable length.

Response rates are high, because the new car owners are motivated by their interest in the subject. Government organisations and companies such as British Gas enjoy good response rates to postal surveys as their 'official' status means that many respondents believe they have an obligation to respond.

Not all subjects are as interesting as cars and not all organisations have the authority of British Gas, and on these occasions an administered interview may be required. Respondents receiving a questionnaire through the post enquiring about the type of pen they use would most probably yield a low response (less than 5 per cent is likely), because the subject is not compelling. This fundamental point means that researchers should avoid using postal surveys except when respondents are highly motivated to answer.

The quality of the sample frame

Postal surveys depend on suitable databases containing the correct names and addresses of respondents. If lists are out of date, contain inaccuracies in spelling of the names and addresses, or are made up of unsuitable respondents, the questionnaires will fall on stony ground and the response rates will be low. Returned and unopened envelopes will indicate that there are problems with the mailing list and could indicate the need for a check back to find out the true reply rate among valid respondents. Whilst check backs are useful, they substantially add to the cost and complexity of the study.

The length of the questionnaire

The shorter the questionnaire, the more likely it will be completed and returned. However, 40 questions carefully laid out on two sides of A3 (folded to make four pages of A4) can look less than 20 questions spread over six single pages. Also, the number of questions does not influence responses as much as the interest factor and there are many examples of questionnaires the size of booklets obtaining high response rates.

Incentives

Respondents want to feel that their efforts in completing the questionnaire are valued. It is important, therefore, that the cover letter gives purpose to the study and convinces recipients that their replies really matter. Legitimacy influences response rates in all types of surveys and it is especially important in postal studies. If possible a benefit should be mentioned such as the promise of better products, improved service or a gift.

All manner of gifts can work. A pen enclosed with the questionnaire is always highly appropriate (it saves searching around for one) and it creates an obligation since to accept it without returning the questionnaire creates a sense of guilt in many people. Equally, some researchers like to encourage respondents to return the questionnaire before they are sent a gift. Prize draws and money vouchers are tried and trusted favourites. Sometimes (generally in business-to-business studies) the offer of a summary of the findings can boost the response.

The layout of the questionnaire

As in all other questionnaires the postal questionnaire must be orderly and logical – but more so. A poor questionnaire can still be made to work if it is administered by a skilled interviewer. However, a questionnaire that arrives through the post has to stand alone with no one at hand to provide advice, answer queries or ensure that the respondent understands what really was meant by the question. Postal questionnaires must be as near perfect as possible with clear questions, clear instructions and adequate room to write in the answer.

The questionnaire should begin with easy questions. Once respondents have answered the first question there is a good chance that they will complete the rest. A difficult question at an early juncture is off-putting.

Ideally, the questionnaire should be desktop published and of good print quality. The more professional the production, the greater will be the response. The use of colour, an attractive layout and the interesting use of white space will all encourage replies. (There are exceptions to these rules; questionnaires that look as if they have been knocked up on an old typewriter have been known to yield high responses because they look hand crafted and not part of a mass mailing).

Some postal surveys require respondent details (name, address and the like) and if these can be completed in advance by the computer, it personalises the document and creates a sense of ownership, removing at least one chore.

The convenience factor

We have emphasised that successful postal questionnaires should be easy to complete. Wherever possible questions should have pre-coded answers simply requiring a box to be ticked or a number circled. Everything should make it easy for respondents to reply. A reply paid envelope will raise response rates. Reply envelopes, affixed with stamps, yield a higher response than those using a business reply service as respondents are inhibited from throwing away unused stamps.

Anonymity

Postal surveys that offer anonymity have a higher response than those where respondents must identify themselves. Much depends on the circumstances. In many business-to-business surveys, respondents may be happy to be identified as long as they are confident that the research is bona fide and not a surreptitious attempt at selling. So too, householders like to be assured that their names will not be sold on to a mailing house and that there will be no sales pressure to follow.

A second mailing

Response rates can be boosted by a second mailing. If the first mailing yields a 25 per cent response, a second one could draw a further 10–15 per cent. The researcher needs, therefore, to consider whether to send a second mailing to the non-respondents and accept the fall off in response rate, or to draw up an extension to the first sample and achieve a 25 per cent response from a fresh list.

Much depends on the importance of winning a high overall response rate. If a high rate from the given sample is critical, then a second mailing is justified and should take place about two weeks after the first. Time could, of course, be a prohibiting factor as the second mailing, together with the waiting time for the responses to come in, will add at least a further four weeks to the survey. It is preferable, though not essential, that the second mailing misses out those who have already returned a questionnaire. Eliminating the initial replies requires respondents to have identified themselves. Also, it is laborious removing respondents from the list if there are hundreds of names and addresses on the sample frame.

The timing of the mailing

There are times of the year when a mailing will yield a poor response. The August holiday month and Christmas are obvious periods to avoid. It is worth trying to avoid any day of the week when people may be extra busy or distracted. On these grounds Monday is a bad day as people face a mountain of work for the week ahead. Friday could also be a poor day for if the questionnaire is not completed immediately, it could be forgotten over the weekend.

DESIGNING COVER LETTERS FOR POSTAL QUESTIONNAIRES

The cover letter accompanying the questionnaire is as important as the questionnaire itself. Wherever possible the name of the respondent should be used on the letter to create a sense of ownership and build the relationship, which is crucial to a good response. Some words of caution. Unless there is absolute certainty about the name and position of the respondent, it is better to address the letter to 'The householder' or, in the case of business-to-business surveys, a functional title such as 'The Production Manager' or 'The Office Equipment Buyer'. Misspelling a name or using the name of someone who has long since left the company is worse than having no name at all.

Rules for writing good cover letters are as follows.

- Explain the purpose of the survey and why the respondent has been selected.
- Give the respondent a reason for wanting to complete the questionnaire: offer a benefit of one kind or another.
- Give clear instructions as to what should be done: how to fill it in, *and* how to send it back.
- Give an assurance that completing the questionnaire is easy.
- If it is possible to do so, give an assurance that replies will be confidential.
- Thank the respondent.

An example of a cover letter and accompanying questionnaire for a postal survey is provided in the following pages.

USING THE PHONE TO BOOST THE RESPONSE

A phone call in advance of sending out the questionnaires can sometimes double response rates. An advance phone call could also be used to collect some of the anecdotal comment which is difficult to obtain in a self-completion questionnaire. In our experience, a

BUSINESS
& MARKET
RESEARCH
—— P L C ——

BUXTON ROAD. HIGH LANE VILLAGE, STOCKPORT, CHESHIRE SK6 8DX
TELEPHONE (0663) 765115 FAX (0663) 762362

Dear Student

As a result of a Bill currently going through the British Parliament, polytechnics in the UK will be redesignated as universities later this year. The consequent change of name, for those of us who are in cities which already contain well established universities, could produce some difficulties. Retaining the name of Manchester in the title is very important because the City has proved such an attraction to students in the past. However, the new name has to make us distinctive from neighbouring sister institutions and several possibilities have been discussed.

This is more than just a name change; it is a re-positioning of Manchester Polytechnic in the field of education. Any change in status will affect you. As part of the consultative process, I would be grateful if you would give the following questions your serious attention. It should not take more than a few minutes of your time as the questionnaire has been designed to be quickly and easily answered.

There are no right or wrong answers to the questions so please just put down what you feel is correct for you.

May I conclude by pointing out that there is no space to record your name and so your reply will be absolutely anonymous. However, we are sampling only a fraction of the people at the Polytechnic and so every questionnaire we hand out we would like returned. We are working to a tight timetable and need your reply by Friday at the latest. Please complete it straight away and place it in one of the boxes close to the entry of your building.

Thank you in anticipation for your help.

Yours sincerely

Paul Hague
Director
29 January 1992

Learning Resources
Centre

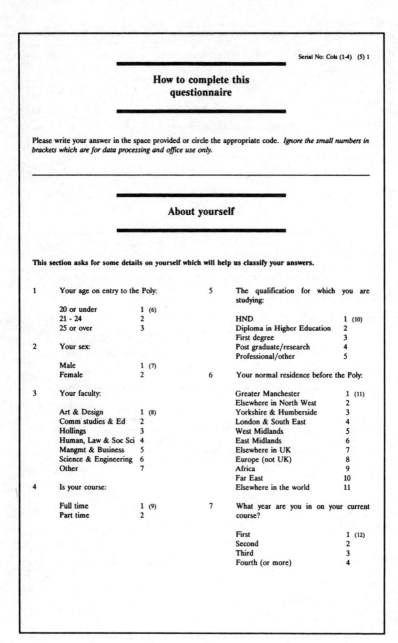

Serial No: Cols (1-4)   (5) 1

How to complete this questionnaire

Please write your answer in the space provided or circle the appropriate code. *Ignore the small numbers in brackets which are for data processing and office use only.*

About yourself

This section asks for some details on yourself which will help us classify your answers.

1   Your age on entry to the Poly:

   20 or under   1 (6)
   21 - 24   2
   25 or over   3

2   Your sex:

   Male   1 (7)
   Female   2

3   Your faculty:

   Art & Design   1 (8)
   Comm studies & Ed   2
   Hollings   3
   Human, Law & Soc Sci   4
   Mangmt & Business   5
   Science & Engineering 6
   Other   7

4   Is your course:

   Full time   1 (9)
   Part time   2

5   The qualification for which you are studying:

   HND   1 (10)
   Diploma in Higher Education   2
   First degree   3
   Post graduate/research   4
   Professional/other   5

6   Your normal residence before the Poly:

   Greater Manchester   1 (11)
   Elsewhere in North West   2
   Yorkshire & Humberside   3
   London & South East   4
   West Midlands   5
   East Midlands   6
   Elsewhere in UK   7
   Europe (not UK)   8
   Africa   9
   Far East   10
   Elsewhere in the world   11

7   What year are you in on your current course?

   First   1 (12)
   Second   2
   Third   3
   Fourth (or more)   4

Your rating of
Manchester Polytechnic

This section explores your attitudes to Manchester Polytechnic.

8   Which *two* factors had most influence on your coming to Manchester Polytechnic?

First factor   .... (13 - 15)

Second factor   .... (16 - 18)

9   Now you are a student at Manchester Polytechnic you may feel able to rate it on various features. Please work through the following list giving Manchester Polytechnic a score out of 5 for each feature. (5 is very good and 1 is very poor). Write your score on the line opposite the feature. If you feel you cannot rate the feature, leave it blank.

The courses at Manchester Polytechnic

Content of the courses	_____	(19)
Promotion of the courses	_____	(20)

Location

Manchester as an enjoyable place	_____	(21)
Manchester as a cultural place	_____	(22)
Friendliness of Manchester people	_____	(23)

The facilities of Manchester Polytechnic

The buildings	_____	(24)
Libraries	_____	(25)
Students' Union	_____	(26)
Dining facilities	_____	(27)
Halls of residence	_____	(28)
Computing facilities	_____	(29)
Other equipment	_____	(30)
Sports facilities	_____	(31)

The teaching staff at Manchester Polytechnic

Teaching skills	_____	(32)
Practical experience	_____	(33)
Academic qualifications	_____	(34)
Caring attitude	_____	(35)

Academic standards of Manchester Polytechnic

Reputation amongst employers	_____	(36)
Reputation amongst friends	_____	(37)

Social life at Manchester Polytechnic

Friendliness	_____	(38)
Clubs and societies	_____	(39)
Student's social life	_____	(40)

Career advantage of Manchester Polytechnic

Long term relevance to career	_____	(41)

Your preferences for other polytechnics or universities

This question is to find out the polytechnics and universities which were in competition with Manchester Polytechnic.

10   Thinking about all the places you really wanted to study, *irrespective of whether they offered you a place or not*, was Manchester Polytechnic your:

           First choice   1 (42)
           Second choice   2
           Third or lower choice   3

11   On the dotted lines below, please list two other colleges, polytechnics or universities, which were your preferred alternatives if you had not come to Manchester Polytechnic.

           First alternative   .... (43 - 50)

           Second alternative   .... (51 - 57)

Repeat cols (1 - 4) Col (5) 2

Your rating of a new name

This final question is to determine your preference for a new name for Manchester Polytechnic.

12   Please consider a number of new names which have been proposed for Manchester Polytechnic and give each a score out of 5 (5 is high, 1 is low) for your views on its "student appeal", its "quality image", and its "appropriateness". In taking into consideration the name, please also consider the initials and colloquialism by which you think the institution will eventually be known.

	Student Appeal	Quality Image	Appropriateness
All Saints University Of Manchester (ASUM)	_____ (6)	_____ (17)	_____ (28)
City of Manchester University (CMU)	_____ (7)	_____ (18)	_____ (29)
Greater Manchester University (GMU)	_____ (8)	_____ (19)	_____ (30)
John Dalton University of Manchester (JDUM)	_____ (9)	_____ (20)	_____ (31)
Manchester All Saints University (MASU)	_____ (10)	_____ (21)	_____ (32)
Manchester City University (MCU)	_____ (11)	_____ (22)	_____ (33)
Manchester Grosvenor University (MGU)	_____ (12)	_____ (23)	_____ (34)
Manchester John Dalton University (MJDU)	_____ (13)	_____ (24)	_____ (35)
Manchester Metropolitan University (MMU)	_____ (14)	_____ (25)	_____ (36)
Manchester Polytechnic (ie same name)	_____ (15)	_____ (26)	_____ (37)
Manchester Queens/Queen Elizabeth University (MQU)	_____ (16)	_____ (27)	_____ (38)

13   If you would like to suggest an alternative name for Manchester Polytechnic, please do so on the dotted line below.

      .... (39 - 49)

Post your questionnaire in the ballot box at the entrance to a main building by Friday, the 31st January.

respondent who has already invested time in helping out with a preliminary telephone interview will be more likely to complete and return a postal questionnaire or one sent by fax. An advance phone call could boost response rates by over 20 per cent to give an overall yield of 40 per cent or more.

Quite clearly there are cost implications attached to using the phone to build response to a postal survey and it may be impractical for a 'do your own' researcher (who may well be using postal research because it is considered the only practical approach given limited resources).

TYPES OF QUESTIONS SUITED (AND NOT SUITED) TO POSTAL QUESTIONNAIRES

Pre-coded questions are suited to postal questionnaires as they save the respondent time writing in the answers. Scalar questions are highly applicable to postal questionnaires because they can be completed quickly by ticking boxes.

The researcher needs to have a good background on a subject to design a workable self-completion questionnaire with sensible pre-coded answers. For example, it would not be possible to construct the following question without some previous knowledge of pipe lagging manufacturers. (And this question is as complicated as it should be in a postal questionnaire.)

Which of the companies listed below would you say has the widest range of pipe lagging products? TICK ONE COMPANY ONLY IN COLUMN A.

And which company has the smallest range? TICK ONE COMPANY ONLY IN COLUMN B.

	Column A Widest Range	Column B Smallest Range
Jiffy	[]	[]
Climatube	[]	[]
Jetlag	[]	[]
Tublite	[]	[]
Armaflex	[]	[]
Insultube	[]	[]
Don't know	[]	[]

Open-ended questions are badly answered in postal surveys. Questions that ask for free-ranging explanations get inadequate (and often illegible) answers. Typical replies are 'because it is good', 'we have always bought it', 'it does its job', etc and there is no opportunity to find out why it is good, why they always buy it or in what way it does its job.

Nor is it possible to ask complicated questions in postal questionnaires. It is no good asking builders' merchants for a detailed breakdown of their purchases of pipe lagging products over the last year because such information will almost certainly need respondents to dig in their files. Such effort can not be assumed from the respondents. The researcher stands some chance if lists of pre-coded answers are provided as this indicates to respondents that an approximation is all that is required.

Finally, about how much did your branch spend on all types of pipe lagging in the last complete year?

Under £1000	[ ]
£1000 to £20,000	[ ]
£20,001 to £50,000	[ ]
Over £50,000	[ ]

In a postal questionnaire it is not possible to disclose information in a controlled fashion (as in a telephone or visit interview) because respondents probably will read ahead and become aware of forthcoming questions. In an administered questionnaire, the name of the sponsor, for example, may be disclosed towards the end, sometimes with special questions to find out more about attitudes to that company. Such unveiling cannot be used in a self-completion questionnaire.

Complicated routing must be avoided in postal surveys. Skipping questions creates confusion and lead to errors in completion.

THE COSTS OF POSTAL SURVEYS

A postal survey is made up of a number of different costs of which postal charges account for nearly 40 per cent of the total, depending, of course, on the response rate achieved. Table 6.1 illustrates the relative importance of each cost based on the buying in of all services, including typing, folding and inserting the mailshot. Excluded from the table is the cost of a purchased list. Lists are not expensive and can range from upwards of around £100 per 1000 names and addresses. Of course, the use of a directory that is already available in the office has no cost of purchase though there would be some costs in abstracting the data.

Table 6.1 *Breakdown of costs in mailing 1000 postal questionnaires*

Cost centre	Percentage of total cost
Outward post	31
Return post (20 per cent response)	7
Typing/folding/inserting	15
Printing the questionnaire (2 sides of A4)	13
Printed reply-paid envelopes	10
Typesetting of questionnaire	10
Printed cover letter	7
Outward envelopes	7
Total	**100**

Table 6.2 shows the comparative costs (in index form) of postal, telephone and face-to-face interviews in a business-to-business situation – say a survey of plumbers or electricians. Inevitably the costs are only a guide as they depend on the number of interviews, who they are with, and the nature of the interview itself. In many circumstances postal questionnaires would be unsuitable as they would not allow sufficient probing of answers. Bearing in mind all these difficulties of comparison, it is evident that there is no great difference in cost between postal and telephone research but both are much cheaper than business-to-business visit interviews.

Table 6.2 *Comparative costs per valid response of different interview methods*

Type of interview	Index of cost per effective interview
Postal survey (assumes 20 per cent response)	100
Telephone interview	100–125
Face-to-face interview	800–1000

PLANNING A POSTAL SURVEY

The watch-words in planning a postal survey are *attention to detail* to ensure that nothing goes wrong. Things to watch out for are:

- Missing out a key question.
- Lack of clarity in the questions.
- Undue complications in the questions or the routings.
- Spelling or grammatical errors on the questionnaire or cover letter.
- Failing to enclose the cover letter, questionnaire and reply-paid envelope.
- Failing to give precise instructions to respondents on how to fill in the questionnaire or how to return it.
- Insufficient funds in the mailing machine to frank all the letters.
- Timing the launch badly such as sending it out during a holiday period or when respondents (in business) are away at an exhibition.

Below is a checklist of things to do in planning a postal survey:

Key tasks	✓	Things to check
Order the list of respondents.		Can it be obtained on disk?
Book help for typing, folding, inserting and franking.		Work out number of people required by estimating time to do each task.
Obtain quotes from printers for questionnaire, cover letter and reply-paid envelopes.		Check quality of paper. Check on turn around time.
Design questionnaire and cover letter.		Obtain approval of client.
Test questionnaire by watching half a dozen colleagues complete it.		Do they understand the questions, do they follow instructions?

Order stationery and printed material – outward envelopes, letterhead, reply-paid envelopes, questionnaire.		Check licence number for reply-paid envelope is up to date. Check that envelopes are of the right size for holding the return questionnaire and assembly of out-bound pieces.
Arrange for the franking machine to be filled.		Note that the Post Office offers a franking service for large quantities of mail.
Brief staff who will be helping with typing and stuffing envelopes.		Arrange for checking a sample of each person's work to see it is being done correctly.
Advise Post Office if there are quantities of over 1000.		You may need to open an account with the PO.
Mail.		Try to plan for the questionnaire to be received on Tuesday (Monday is busy after the weekend and the rest of the week is available for filling it in).
Brief staff who deal with incoming mail on requirements for opening (or not opening) the returned questionnaires.		Is there a necessity to check the franked return questionnaire to determine the location of the respondent?
Track numbers of responses each day to determine when to close the survey.		Consider data processing after two weeks or re-mailing with a reminder.

7

Telephone Interviewing

We turn now to practical advice on carrying out a programme of telephone interviewing: how to plan and achieve successful interviews over the phone. First we look at the advantages and disadvantages of the approach, particularly against face-to-face interviewing.

THE ROLE OF TELEPHONE INTERVIEWING

The greatest advantages of the telephone against face-to-face interviewing are its speed and low cost. These are most evident in business-to-business market research.

In favourable circumstances, perhaps five to six 20 minute interviews with managers in industry can be completed in a day over the telephone. In the same time only one or two interviews could be achieved face-to-face. The difference in costs between visits and telephone interviews, therefore, primarily reflects the greater productivity of the latter and also the fact that telephone charges are considerably less than travel and out-of-pocket expenses.

In consumer research the time and cost advantages of telephone interviewing are not quite so clear-cut. If the comparison is between street and telephone interviewing then there is probably little difference in either time or cost – in fact, street interviewing might even be cheaper. However, when compared with household interviews, the telephone is both quicker and cheaper since there is no time wasted in travel between interview points.

A strong argument in favour of telephone interviewing in business-to-business market research is that virtually anyone targeted for interview is likely to be accessible by phone. This is not the case in consumer markets, nor is phone interviewing as well accepted. Business-to-business respondents accept the phone as part and parcel of their daily lives, while to many a householder it is an intrusion into their resting or social hours. On the other hand concerns about doorstep security favour the telephone as a consumer interviewing medium. Householders do not have to answer the door to a stranger, while interviewers are saved the risk of entering dubious neighbourhoods.

ARGUMENTS AGAINST TELEPHONE INTERVIEWS

We have seen that there are a number of strong arguments in favour of telephone interviews, with particularly important benefits in cost and speed. However, there are sometimes good reasons for *not* using telephone interviews.

Visuals are difficult to use

If something has to be shown, then the telephone is not the right approach. However, telephone interviews may still have a role to play, feeding in information to a wider project. For example, in new product research, data on current methods of using or consuming products may be required and this could be obtained over the telephone, leaving face-to-face interviews to test the new concept.

With some imagination, means can be devised of carrying out interviews using more than one approach such as phone/fax/phone or phone/letter/phone. By splitting the interview in this way, visuals can be used in a telephone interviewing programme and the researcher can obtain an amalgam of say an hour of respondents' time without taxing their patience at one sitting and at a lower cost than via visits.

Prompted questions

It is sometimes necessary to ask respondents to consider a number of predetermined factors in order to test their views. More than five or six factors on a list are difficult to hold in the mind and so it is usual in face-to-face interviews to show these on a card so that they can be given fair consideration. Clearly, the phone makes it difficult to ask such lengthy, prompted questions.

Unconsidered responses

The telephone forces instant responses to questions. Sometimes the instant response may be what is wanted but at other times a question may require the respondent to reflect.

Interview length

Telephone interviewing is, on the whole, better suited to shorter interviews and 10 to 15 minutes or so is probably the ideal length. Face-to-face interviews are usually longer and in business-to-business situations, a visit interview of less than half an hour would probably be regarded as more suited to the telephone (all other things permitting).

Interview depth

In telephone interviews the questions and answers are generally kept short and so the medium is not ideal for depth interviewing. It does not encourage long and discursive responses. Furthermore, the lack of personal contact prohibits the interviewer assessing respondents and obtaining an extra feel for what is behind the reply.

Despite these limitations, the advantages of telephone interviewing are still enormous and, with exceptions such as new product research, the 'do your own' researcher will find many applications for this most important tool.

PLANNING

A well planned and structured questionnaire is crucial to a telephone interview. The interviewer must be able to put the questions fluently, the questions have to be simple and clear, and they must flow in an effective sequence. In other words, the questionnaire should be designed to suit the medium.

Where more than one interviewer is to work on a telephone survey, a formal briefing session is needed so that the team can be told the background to the research and the questionnaire can be explained in detail. Interviewers must be wholly familiar with the questions before they begin, and in this respect telephone and face-to-face interviewing are no different.

In telephone interviewing, a directory of one kind or another may be used to obtain the sample. In the case of consumer research, the 'white pages' of the telephone directories are an excellent frame from which to choose the random sample. However, some points should be borne in mind about using the telephone directory in this way.

- The telephone directory is not a comprehensive sample frame as it probably covers only 60 per cent of the domestic population;

exclusions include the sizable proportion of subscribers who are ex-directory as well as those not on the phone at all. In business-to-business markets researchers are handicapped by the absence of one comprehensive source of companies. However, there are many relevant commercial directories such as *Yellow Pages* and *Kompass* (see Chapter 3).

- The 'white pages' telephone directory is better thought of as a list of households than of individuals and an additional procedure will be needed to select specific respondents within a home. For example, instructions would be needed for interviewers to obtain a specified quota of people who are male, female, of a certain social class, etc.

- Until contact is made, nothing is known about the respondents at the other end of the line. This may mean a high ratio of contacts to interviews if the respondent has to qualify for interview by, for example, ownership of a particular product or some personal characteristic. By contrast, the face-to-face interviewer can sometimes use observation to screen suitable respondents. For example, in a survey on lawn care products the face-to-face interviewer knows there is little point approaching houses without gardens. Similarly, if interviewers in the street require a sample of females aged over 40, they could use observation to select appropriate respondents. Clearly the telephone prohibits these vital initial screens.

It is desirable in telephone interviewing to keep contact sheets that provide a record of all calls made (rather than just the successful interviews). At the end of the interviewing programme, these contact sheets show who did *not* qualify for interview, who refused and if a respondent was not available. An analysis of the contact sheets may provide useful research findings such as the incidence of usage of a product. The design of the contact sheets can be varied to suit the needs of specific jobs but the usual format is a line for each contact and columns to record the outcome of calls.

Records should also be kept of the costs incurred, specifically the telephone charges. In most surveys it is necessary to account for all costs so that a post mortem on the project can show how close it ran to budget. Over time, records of costings can help when budgeting future work.

Telephone costs are based on time and call bands related to distance. Costs can therefore be calculated by timing each call and multiplying by the appropriate rate. Costings calculated in this way are, however, a chore and, if telephone interviewing on any scale is undertaken, it is far better to have the phones monitored by meters or a computer link. The cost is quite modest and it means that units are automatically recorded on each call or per interviewing session.

Respondent's name	Address	Date/time of calling			Result	
Job Number:_____ Project Title: _____						
		1st call	2nd call	3rd call	Interview (✓)	Reason for non-interview

Figure 7.1 *Example of Contact Sheet*

A final aspect of planning telephone interviews is setting call objectives – that is the number of interviews that should be achieved in a day. What is realistic depends on the following factors.

- *The nature of the respondents and the difficulty of contacting them.*
  If it is necessary to interview respondents who are only available at particular times, the strike rate will be less than for respondents who are always at their desk. Farmers, for example, are away from a phone for most of their working day and are most easily interviewed early in the morning, at lunchtime or early evening.

Dentists are in the surgery ten hours or more a day but are only available for interview for half an hour during that time. People in business are always in meetings and are increasingly hard to pin down as delayering and down-sizing has put everyone under more pressure!

- *Respondent's qualification for interview.* If respondents have to meet a tight specification of qualifications before they can be interviewed, this will cut back the number of interviews that can be achieved per day. In consumer research, for example, the respondent may have to own or buy a certain product or fall within a particular demographic grouping.
- *Interview duration.* Whether the interview will take just five minutes or half an hour has an obvious effect on the number of interviews that can be carried out in a day and their cost.

Bearing these points in mind, five to six successful interviews per day among business-to-business respondents is considered good, despite a theoretical maximum of up to twenty.

TELEPHONE MANNERS

In telephone interviews respondents are asked to give up their time and part with information to an unknown person at the end of a line. Interviewers' success in such situations depends very much on their approach.

A successful interviewing approach starts before even picking up the phone; the interviewer must adopt a positive manner. Here are a few suggestions.

- *Resolve to project a positive attitude.* Make it sound as though you want the respondent to talk to you. Hesitancy may suggest a lack of legitimacy and result in the respondent being unhelpful.
- *Similarly, sound interested in the project.* Sometimes the subject matter of research is pedestrian, if not downright boring, but this should not be communicated to respondents. If you don't sound interested, how can you expect cooperation?
- *Don't talk too quickly.* In your eagerness you may be tempted to speak with the rapidity of a machine gun in order to complete the interview as quickly as possible. The chances are that you will sound garbled and the respondent will be turned off.
- *Be courteous.* A courteous and genial interviewer will encourage a similar response from the other person.

- *Stick to the questionnaire.* You should be using a questionnaire, however simple the interview. Stick to the questionnaire and commit to asking *all* the questions. This applies even if you designed the questionnaire.
- *Using a questionnaire means listening* to the respondent as well as asking the questions. Never finish a sentence for respondents or assume you know what they are about to say.

CONTACTING THE RIGHT RESPONDENT

The interview will only be worthwhile if the respondent is qualified to answer the questions. The precise description of who should be interviewed will have been decided at the planning stage and it is only now, at the time of interviewing, that the problem becomes one of actually finding these respondents.

In consumer research the problem of finding the right person is usually not very acute. Sometimes target respondents are defined simply as any adult, with equal quotas of men and women. Alternatively, the respondents may have to own or have bought something, but this will be resolved through the initial questions. In either case, finding the relevant respondent is not difficult once you are through to their home.

The situation is more problematical in business-to-business market research where the respondent may be defined in terms of their responsibility for some function or activity, for example:

- The person responsible for choosing the make of trucks in the company's fleet.
- The person with day-to-day responsibility for the company's computer operations.

Often these responsibilities can be equated with a specific job title, in the examples above perhaps the transport manager and information technology manager. However, job titles vary widely between companies. In some cases the specific responsibility may be that of a manager with wide interests. In practice, therefore, the job title may only be a guide to the appropriate respondent and as soon as possible their specific responsibility should be checked by questions, such as 'Who decides the make of vehicles used by your company?' The questionnaire should include such 'qualifying' questions.

Another point to remember about business-to-business surveys is that most respondents are reached through a receptionist. Quite often receptionists do not know who in their company is responsible for a specific function and, anxious to get rid of the caller as quickly as possible, connect you to the wrong person. Generally, it is better therefore to ask for someone by job title and, if necessary, be prepared to go through two or more potential respondents before finding the right one.

Some other points about dealing with receptionists are:

- As well as asking for the 'transport manager' (or whoever), ask the receptionist for the person's name before being put through. This means that the respondent can be addressed personally from the outset.
- It is better not to discuss in any detail with other people the reasons for wanting to speak to a respondent. Too much knowledge about the questions which lie in store may cause the receptionist to decide that the respondent does not 'want to be bothered' by a market research enquiry.

When the prospective respondents are senior managers, the telephone interviewer may have to hurdle a secretary whose job includes making sure the boss is not pestered with trivial phone calls. Here, skill and politeness are the essential ingredients for getting through to the respondent. Secretaries can be allies and help win the interview but they must be treated with respect and taken into the confidence of the interviewer.

INITIAL CONTACT WITH THE RESPONDENT

Generally, respondents decide whether or not they are going to cooperate within the first minute of the contact. The opening gambit is therefore vital.

Once through to the respondent it is important to make it clear that this is a market research exercise that will not result in any sales pressure.

> Hello Mr Jones. This is… I am trying to find out what people think of various types of heavy trucks and I wondered if you would be kind enough to spare me a few minutes.

With a simple introduction such as this, many respondents will be willing to cooperate without further discussion and it is possible to move on to the first question. Not all respondents can be won over so easily and the interviewer must be ready to meet objections that may be raised. Suggestions for countering objections are given in Chapter 8.

DURING THE INTERVIEW

Once a respondent has agreed to go ahead, things usually proceed smoothly. It is uncommon for a respondent to return to any objections or to end the interview prematurely.

During the interview the respondent must be kept on course, the interviewer maintaining the initiative and projecting a positive manner even if the questionnaire is long and wearisome.

The temptation must be avoided to miss out questions because the respondent is showing signs of impatience. The respondent's interest must be maintained by encouragement and assurances that the responses are valuable.

Where necessary, it is legitimate to depart from the script of the questionnaire to indicate that the interview is nearing the end. Normally the questions are asked in the way they are written down but additional non-committal comments at the end of responses can be used as acknowledgement. These are the pleasantries which lubricate general conversation:

- Oh, yes.
- Yes, thank you.
- Right.

AT THE END OF THE INTERVIEW

The objective at the end of the interview is to leave the respondent as happy as possible without any regrets for having helped. If the respondent feels disgruntled and that he has been 'tricked' into participating, he will probably react negatively in future encounters with interviewers. In the long run, all market researchers are dependent on continuing cooperation. Also it may be necessary to go back to the respondent to check out some points at the time the data is being analysed.

Here are a few suggestions on how to finish the interview in the best way.

- As you reach the last or next to last question indicate that this is the case. The respondent can start to relax before the final sign off.

- Thank the respondent, for example 'Thank you Mr... That is all I wanted to ask you. Your comments have been very useful.'
- Reassure the respondent that he or she has participated in a market research survey and that their responses will be used for that purpose only; for example 'This is a market research survey and the information you have given me will not be used for any other purpose.'

When the interview is finished, quickly check over the questionnaire. In the heat of the moment, responses are often scribbled down and it is better to tidy up immediately. In particular:

- Check that the name of the respondent, their company (if business-to-business market research) and the telephone number have been recorded.
- Make sure that all the responses for 'closed' questions have been completed. Where the question calls for a single response, check there is only one.
- Check that any 'shorthand' used to record open-ended questions is expanded to a full and legible record.
- Where relevant, check that any units of value (eg weights, dimensions) are clearly stated.

Checking over the questionnaires in this way can save a lot of problems later on.

8

Face-To-Face Interviewing

Face-to-face interviewing is the traditional and still the most common method of collecting market research data. It leads telephone and postal research as a primary data collection method though it has lost some ground in recent years to telephone interviewing. In this chapter we look at the applications for face-to-face interviewing and consider when this technique is appropriate. Advice is given on how to get respondents to agree to be interviewed in the first place and then how to maintain cooperation as the questioning unfolds. The differences between consumer and business-to-business face-to-face interviews are also discussed.

ADVANTAGES OF FACE-TO-FACE INTERVIEWING

Face-to-face interviews are still the most common means of collecting primary information for good reasons.

Better explanations

In a face-to-face interview, the interviewer can gain a deeper understanding of the validity of a response. Respondents are able to provide better explanations as they have more time to consider their answers. Sometimes interviewers need to show advertisements, logos, headlines or samples and this is plainly suited to face-to-face situations.

Depth

It is easier to maintain the interest of respondents for a longer period of time in face-to-face interviews. Being face-to-face with respondents gives the interviewer more control and refusals to answer questions are less likely than those over the telephone. Concern about confidentiality can be more readily satisfied than with an 'anonymous' person at the end of a phone. An interviewer on the doorstep or in the High Street can show an identity card.

Greater accuracy

In a face-to-face interview respondents can look up information and products can be examined. If the interview is at business premises, files of information can be referred to, or phone calls made to colleagues to confirm a point. The interviewer may be able to make a visual check to ensure that the answers are correct.

Product placements

Product placements can be sent through the post but it is usually better for them to be delivered by hand by the interviewer. Being face-to-face with respondents permits a more thorough briefing on how to use the product. Pre-test questions can be asked, and arrangements can be made for the follow-up.

DISADVANTAGES OF FACE-TO-FACE INTERVIEWING

Against the advantages of face-to-face interviewing, there are a number of disadvantages.

Organisation

Face-to-face interviews are difficult to organise. If the face-to-face interviews are country-wide and the sample is of any size, a national field force is required. The subject may be complex and demand a personal briefing, which is expensive, time-consuming and awkward to arrange when interviewers are scattered geographically. (There are nearly always some interviewers who cannot make the briefing and separate arrangements need to be made for them.) When the interviewing is complete, there is a logistical problem of collecting all the questionnaires. It is not unusual for a large survey to be held up by one or two interviewers who are late returning their completed questionnaires.

Quality control

Where a team of interviewers is used for a programme of personal interviews, quality control becomes an issue. The interviews need to be done in a uniform way and there is always some danger of individual interviewers skimping their work. Various quality control methods can be used such as check-backs to respondents, but this adds to the costs and complexity of the project.

Cost

The cost of face-to-face consumer interviews varies considerably between those carried out in the street and the home. Household interviews based on pre-selected samples are, in turn, more expensive than those to a quota. In general, street interviews cost the same to carry out as telephone interviews. In some cases, street interviews offer advantages over the telephone by allowing show cards and visuals, while at other times the facility to random sample and achieve complete geographical coverage could swing the benefits in favour of telephone interviewing.

A comparison between face-to-face and other methods of data collection must take into consideration *all costs*. Face-to-face interviewing may use interviewers employed at the same rates as (say) telephone interviewing, but work in the field incurs expense. Allowances have to be made for bringing people together for briefings if these are required, and to this must be added out-of-pocket expenses for sustenance, travel and post. In business-to-business studies, face-to-face interviews often cost ten times those carried out by telephone.

Time

Face-to-face interviews are time consuming because of the travel time between respondents (except, of course, when the interviews are carried out in the street). The prior commitments of the interviewers and the delays caused by questionnaires being mailed out and returned normally mean that at least a two-week period is necessary for organising a face-to-face interviewing project. A month is more reasonable. A programme of business-to-business interviews may have less face-to-face interviews than a consumer study but it too takes an inordinate time to organise as the researchers struggle to set up interviews in busy managers' diaries.

CONSUMER FACE-TO-FACE INTERVIEWING

We now consider two of the most important methods of face-to-face interviewing in consumer research: those carried out in the street and those in the home.

Street interviews: applications

Where the people in the street are likely to be the target group. If the subject of the survey is food or shopping, it makes sense that the interviews are carried out close to a busy shopping area.

Where the questionnaire is short and simple. Using a short questionnaire, and assuming that the questions are applicable for most of the passers-by, an interviewer can achieve 30 and sometimes more interviews in a day.

Where the questions appertain to a local issue. A survey investigating a local issue could be suited to street interviewing. Interviewers positioned in a busy town centre would be able to collect the views of local people as they are travelling to work or are out shopping.

Where cost and time are vital issues. Street interviews are quicker, easier to organise and cheaper than house-to-house visits. This consideration will often be very important in 'do your own' research.

Street interviews: limitations

Where the interview is long or complicated. The street is not a place to carry out interviews which take more than five to ten minutes. Shoppers with their arms laden or dashing home are unlikely to cooperate for more than a few minutes.

Where it is necessary to show many visuals. It is difficult to show visuals or prompt cards in a street interview. Respondents may be caught without their glasses, the light may be poor, the rain or wind could cause problems and if the shopper's hands are full, the show cards cannot be held conveniently.

Where the targets for interview are not likely to be around. The street is not the best place to find working people, who, in the main, will be at their offices or factories at times when interviewers are at large. Old people who cannot easily get about, people who are ill, and people who dislike shopping are going to be under represented in street surveys.

HOUSEHOLD INTERVIEWS

The advantages and disadvantages of household interviews are, by and large, the corollaries of those for street interviews. They are nevertheless worth stating to highlight the strengths and weaknesses of the method.

Household interviews: applications

Where the interview is long and complicated. An interview of more than ten to fifteen minutes needs to be carried out at the respondent's home.

Where there are products or visuals to show. Visuals (cards, advertisements, storyboards) need to be shown in a convenient environment. Where there are a number, it may be necessary to lay them out on a table and this requires a home environment. Similarly, demonstration of products needs to be in the home.

Where a random sampling method is used. A true random sample requires a sample frame such as an electoral list of households to select from. Random walk is a commonly used approximation to a true random sample and again it is household based.

Where the questions are of a sensitive nature. If the questions are personal or sensitive in any way, it is better to carry out the interview in the privacy of the respondent's home.

Where the interviewer needs to check out something in the house. Research into (say) domestic appliances may require the interviewer to actually see the product so they can check out details such as the model code.

Household interviews: limitations

Where time and cost are paramount. Household interviews are time-consuming and costly. If the householder is out when the interviewer calls, then usually up to two further attempts have to be made to achieve the interview.

Where the home environment could influence the response. A survey carried out in the home, for example with teenagers on their attitude to drugs could be swayed by fear of an ear-wagging parent. The street is a public place but in certain circumstances it can offer more privacy than the home.

OBTAINING COOPERATION AND CARRYING OUT INTERVIEWS WITH THE PUBLIC

Wherever the interview is carried out, in the street or the home, it is usually with a complete stranger. The interviewer asks this stranger to part with their time, views, facts and opinions, usually with no reward. Often the person may be busy, aggravated by personal problems or resent the intrusion of their privacy. The interviewer has no rights whatsoever to demand cooperation. Everything depends, therefore, on the interviewer's approach.

The first few seconds of contact are critical. Respondents need to feel that they are being asked to take part in a worthwhile project and that they are in the hands of an expert. If the interviewer has an identity card or a letter of authority, it should be shown to the respondent as part of the introduction. In most surveys, the interviewers will be given a script of their opening lines. In this they will probably explain that a survey is being carried out (here emphasising that there is no selling motive involved), which company is carrying out the survey, and the length of time the interview can be expected to take. Rejections can be expected. However, busy people, people who are harassed, and those who cherish privacy could all have important views or buying characteristics valuable to a survey and need to be included to avoid bias. It is up to the interviewer to obtain as high a response rate as possible.

Objections to being interviewed fall into a pattern and can be pre-empted.

The respondent who has no time. The interviewer must make a judgement on this. It is unreasonable to expect a shopper, running for a bus, to miss it for the sake of a survey. However, for many respondents the excuse of no time means insufficient interest and it is up to the interviewer to engage them with a bright and enthusiastic approach.

The respondent believes they can't answer the questions. Some respondents see market research interviews as tests. A good interviewer should be able to alleviate these concerns by explaining that the questions are quite straightforward and there are no right or wrong answers.

The respondent requires confidentiality. These respondents need an assurance that the information will be pooled to draw conclusions and that there is no way of tying answers to individuals. It should be stressed that the survey is for market research purposes only and will not be followed up by a sales approach.

Interviewers can head off these and other objections by acting positively. In winning the interview, the interviewer must be both assumptive and courteous. They should lead with the first question as soon as possible as involvement and interest will safeguard co-operation. Very few respondents abandon an interview once started.

On completion, the interviewer owes the respondent a thank-you. Sometimes a card is given to the respondent which explains who carried out the interview and why. In street interviews it is normal practice to ask the respondent for their name and addresses for quality control purposes. Diplomacy and a special explanation may be needed for people reticent about giving their address to a stranger.

The interview may be complete but the interviewer has not finished. A final check is needed over the basic details. All questions should be legible and answered (or marked as a refusal). The name of the interviewer, the date, and the respondent's name and address should be checked to ensure that they are filled in.

FACE-TO-FACE INTERVIEWING IN BUSINESS SITUATIONS

Researchers interviewing people in business share some of the same problems as consumer interviewers. The confident, courteous, assumptive approach is as relevant here as in the home or the street. None the less, there are some special features of business situations which should be heeded in winning cooperation from respondents.

Obtaining the business-to-business interview

Face-to-face interviews in business-to-business surveys are almost always held at the respondent's place of work and generally by prior appointment made in an initial phone contact. The subject is likely to be work related and quite reasonably the respondent will wish to be assured that, by taking part, it is not compromising his or her employer. Respondents will ask for details about the purpose of the study and on whose behalf the work is being carried out. The researcher should carefully consider how to answer this question, especially if the sponsor wishes to remain anonymous. Working on behalf of the researcher is the fact that people have an interest in their jobs and they are flattered at the opportunity to express their views. Absolute confidence must be displayed in the initial approach. Even so, there will be rejections, which usually happen at initial contact when seeking an interview appointment. Typical reasons for refusal include:

- It is company policy not to take part in surveys.
- We have already taken part in a survey recently.
- I'm too busy right now. Try me again in a few weeks.
- I'm not the person you want to speak to.
- We only do questionnaires through the post. Send it to me and I'll complete it for you.
- You'll have to give me an idea of the questions before I can help you.
- What's in it for me?
- I know the research sponsor and I've told him all that I have to say on the subject.

There are a number of guidelines which will head off any objections and help achieve cooperation.

- *Be brief*. The researcher should come straight to the point. The respondent will become bored with a longwinded introduction and, in any case, it gives time to conceive objections.
- *Be honest*. It helps if the researcher can state who is sponsoring the study, though to minimise bias this disclosure usually takes place at the end of the interview. Under no circumstances should the researcher lie or mislead respondents as to the sponsor or purpose of the study.
- *Justify the study*. The respondent wants to hear that the study is of value and in some way could benefit his or her company. The promise of better service, improved designs or better quality could help rationalise why it is worthwhile spending time answering questions.
- *Give assurances*. The researcher should assure the respondent that the information will be confidential to the market research department or agency. Sometimes it is necessary to provide this assurance in writing.
- *Confirm the interview*. As a courtesy to the respondent, but also to ensure there is no confusion about the date and time of the interview, the researcher should confirm the arrangements by letter or fax.

Conducting the interview

At the time of the interview (and by now the serious objections will have been overcome), the respondent plays host but expects the initiative to be taken by the researcher. Before the questions start, the scene should be set with a short recap as to the purpose of the study. A reiteration of the assurance of confidentiality may ease the respondent's mind.

The interview should begin with some easy questions, perhaps background information on the respondent's company which will be a useful context for answers to come. Very quickly the atmosphere will relax and the respondent will warm to the task of answering more difficult questions. This aspect of the interviewing process needs to be considered earlier when the questionnaire is designed.

Respondents expect researchers to ask questions and record their answers whether on a questionnaire or tape recorder. Taping interviews does not induce the inhibitions that might be imagined. An assumptive and confident manner works best, perhaps introducing the tape recorder as an 'electronic notebook' to compensate for slow writing skills. The respondent will soon forget it is there.

In a face-to-face interview with a business respondent the researcher is able to seek clarification on technical issues. If the researcher is unclear or suspects that a misunderstanding has occurred, questions can be repeated and, if a response seems thin, probing can take place.

At the end of the interview the researcher must close and thank the respondent, and make a note to follow up any promises made in reciprocation. The door should be left open to call back should further information be required when the data are analysed. A thank-you letter costs little in time and money and will help to ensure that other researchers will be cordially received at some future date.

9

Data Analysis and Reporting

Previous chapters have discussed how to collect data through interviews or other sorts of fieldwork. The end result of fieldwork is completed questionnaires or similar records. Except in the case of overview interviews or small scale qualitative research, individual questionnaires are of little value or interest. What is required is aggregated data for the whole sample (or for sub-samples). Data analysis is the process of producing this from the individual responses or 'raw' data. In this chapter data analysis of quantitative survey data is described in some detail with shorter comments on processing the outcome of qualitative research. We then discuss how this data, together with the results of desk research, can be effectively reported and communicated to those who will use it to take decisions.

QUANTITATIVE DATA ANALYSIS OUTPUT

Data analysis is best discussed back to front, ie by considering the output that is sought before going on to how the work can be practically done. To illustrate typical data analysis output we can take as an example research involving 200 interviews using a questionnaire which included the following question:

Q5   How likely are you to buy the appliance in the next two years? Would you say you are...
READ SCALE. ONE RESPONSE ONLY.

Very likely   ☐
Fairly likely   ☐
Neither likely nor unlikely   ☐

Fairly unlikely   ☐
Very unlikely   ☐

The responses from all 200 interviews can be simply shown as the
number giving each response: very likely = 50, fairly likely = 80, and
so on. However, it is better to set out the results in a more formal
manner such as Table 9.1. This gives the responses as percentages
rather than numbers but the total number of responses on which
the percentages are based – the *base number* or sample size – is also
shown. The inclusion of the base number in a table is essential in
presenting survey data since, as discussed in Chapter 4, the accuracy
of a sample is determined by its size. Anyone using the data in the
table needs this information in order to make a judgement on its
reliability. Another point to note about Table 9.1 is that it is
adequately labelled and self explanatory with a clear title and a
definition of which respondents are included, in this case the whole
sample – all respondents.

Table 9.1 *Likelihood of buying appliance in the next two years (all
respondents)*

Likelihood of buying	%
Very likely	25
Fairly likely	40
Neither likely nor unlikely	14
Fairly unlikely	18
Very unlikely	3
Total	**100**
Base (sample size)	200

Possibly, however, it may be useful to present data for just part of
the sample, for example for those respondents who already own
the appliance and show their likelihood of purchase. Often questionnaires include questions that only apply to certain respondents
depending on their responses to earlier questions. The technical
term for this is *filtering* and in Table 9.2 the filter used is existing
owners.

In nearly all quantitative market research, comparisons between
different groups of respondents are required. This is achieved by
cross analysis. Table 9.3 is a simple example of this and compares

the likelihood of purchase between owners and non-owners of the appliance together with the breakdown for the whole sample; the data for all respondents (total), owners and non-owners are shown as separate columns. Two points to note are that the figures in the 'owners' column are the same as in Table 9.2 (which by filtering showed responses just for non-owners) and that a base number – the number of respondents – is shown for each column. Again, the inclusion of base numbers is very important in order to judge the reliability of making comparisons between sub-groups of the sample. In this case the two sub-groups of owners and non-owners each have bases of 100 and at this sample size the range of sampling error is quite high. However, in the example the differences are quite striking and in the statistical sense significant despite the fairly low bases.

Table 9.2 *Likelihood of buying appliance in the next two years (existing owners of the appliance)*

Likelihood of buying	%
Very likely	40
Fairly likely	0
Neither likely nor unlikely	25
Fairly unlikely	30
Very unlikely	5
Total	**100**
Base	100

In Table 9.3 the cross analysis is very simple. It can be far more complex. The likelihood of buying, for example, could be compared (cross analysed) for different demographic groupings such as age, sex, income group, etc and this sort of analysis is almost standard in most consumer market research. Cross analysis can in fact be by any other question included in the questionnaire, although by the same token it is too late at this stage to seek an analysis by a variable or possible question which was not asked. The moral is that planning data analysis needs to start when the questionnaire is designed.

Table 9.3 *Likelihood of buying appliance in the next two years by existing ownership of the appliance (all respondents)*

Likelihood of buying	Total %	Owners %	Non-owners %
Very likely	25	40	10
Fairly likely	40	0	80
Neither likely nor unlikely	14	25	5
Fairly unlikely	18	30	5
Very unlikely	3	5	0
Total	100	100	100
Base	200	100	100

The question we have used is a *scalar* question and a common way of presenting the responses from this type of question is by *mean scores* as shown in Table 9.4. Each score (shown for each column) is a weighted average of the numerical values assigned to the pre-coded responses (+2 for 'very likely', +1 for 'fairly likely', etc) and the numbers of respondents giving each response.* The resulting mean score in the example indicates the average likelihood of purchase for the whole sample and for both owners and non-owners, and with only one figure to consider makes comparisons easy. In the table non-owners appear more likely to buy than owners – a mean score of +0.95 compared to +0.40.

Mean scores can be calculated with a pocket calculator but if more than a few are required the work is tedious. Where the data analysis is carried out by specialised computer software, however, mean scores can be produced automatically. Interpreting scalar data just from mean scores does, though, have some dangers and the (contrived) example in Table 9.4 illustrates this. Comparison of the mean scores of owners and non-owners suggests that it is non-owners who are most likely to buy the appliance. However, if we look at the distribution of responses we see that among owners 40 per cent are very likely to buy compared to only 10 per cent of non-owners, and the higher mean score among non-owners is

---

*   In the example the total mean score is calculated:
      $(2 \times 25 + 1 \times 40) - (1 \times 18 + 2 \times 3) / 100$
      The neither likely nor unlikely response has been given a zero value.

because, compared to owners, far fewer gave a fairly/very unlikely response. Which of these two ways of interpreting the data will give a better indication of future purchase intentions? Whatever the answer it is clear that interpretation based on mean scores alone has limitations and at the most should be regarded as no more than a sometimes useful way of summarising data.

Table 9.4 *Likelihood of buying appliance in the next two years by existing owners of the appliance (all respondents)*

Likelihood of buying	Total %	Owners %	Non-owners %
Very likely (+2)	25	40	10
Fairly likely (+1)	40	0	80
Neither likely nor unlikely (0)	14	25	5
Fairly unlikely (–1)	18	30	5
Very unlikely (–2)	3	5	0
Total	100	100	100
Mean Score	*+0.66*	*+0.40*	*+0.95*
Base	200	100	100

Drawing inferences from a sample to a population requires that the sample is representative – it mirrors the population in at least important characteristics. However, often the achieved sample is not representative and over or under represents population groups. Sometimes this may be by design so that adequate numbers of respondents of each important group are included. Table 9.5 shows the responses from another question in the appliance survey – whether the appliance is owned – and provides a cross analysis by household tenure (owner occupiers and tenants). It will be seen that in the sample, owner occupiers and tenants each accounted for 50 per cent of the sample (sample % across). However, among the population sampled it is known (from other sources) that in fact only 25 per cent are tenants and this group is, therefore, over represented in the sample (and owner occupiers under represented). Possibly this was by design to provide an adequate number of both. Because of the make up of the sample, the total (unweighted) column will not, therefore, be a reliable indication of appliance ownership among the whole population. A solution is to calculate a *weighted* total column. This is the result of multiplying the responses among owner occupiers by a weighting factor* and adding this to the responses from tenants also multiplied by a weighting factor and then re-percentaging the combined values to give the weighted column.

Table 9.5 *Ownership of the appliance by home tenure: weighted totals (all respondents)*

Own appliance	Total		Owner occupiers %	Tenants %
	Unweighted	Weighted		
Yes	43	51	60	25
No	57	49	40	75
Total	100	100	100	100
Sample size	200	200	100	100
Sample (% across)	100		50	50
Population (% across)	100		75	25
Weighting factor			1.50	0.50

Weighting is probably a bit esoteric for 'do your own' market research. In the example weighting was a relatively simple calculation based on only one variable – household tenure. However, in practice, the sample may differ from the population in a number of important aspects (eg age and sex as well as tenure) and several variables may need to be used in weighting to replicate a representative sample. This is beyond any simple calculation but most specialised data processing software is capable of doing this as required once the population breakdown is inputted.

To this point we have considered only the analysis of pre-coded questions. However, questionnaires often include open-ended questions of the type shown below. In principle each response to such a question is unique. The responses given by just nine respondents are shown below the question.

---

*   The weighting factor is calculated by dividing the percentage of the population who are owner occupiers by the percentage among the sample: 75/50 = 1.50. For tenants the corresponding calculation is 25/50 = 0.50.

Q8   Why would you not consider buying the appliance in
      the next two years?
      DO NOT PROMPT. RECORD VERBATIM.

Respondent	Response
1	Too big to go in my kitchen.
2	I cannot afford to buy one.
3	They look so ugly.
4	I don't like the colours and they cost too much.
5	I hear they are unreliable.
6	With only two of us at home we have no need of one.
7	I expect the prices will come down. I will wait until then.
8	I think they are complicated to use.
9	I don't know really.

With only nine responses it is easy to read through them all and
make some generalisations (or not). However, with, say, 100 respondents each giving their own reasons for non-purchase it is
much harder or impossible to see any common pattern. What we
need to do is to group the individual responses into similar categories. This is illustrated below.

Code	Response category	Respondents included
1	Design of appliance	1, 3, 4, 8
2	Cost factors	2, 4, 7
3	Unreliability	5
6	Have no need	6
7	Don't know	9

Each response category is designated a code and if computer analysis is to be used it will be these codes which are inputted. The process
of categorising individual responses to open-ended questions is
called *coding* and the list of codes and categories is a *code frame*. As
can be seen in the example, an individual respondent (4) may give
a response which falls in two categories. Also categorising individual responses involves a certain judgement – in the example four
responses have been grouped as 'design of the appliance'. However,
one mentioned size, one appearance (ugly), one colours and one
difficulty of use. It may be more useful to group these in different
ways (eg design – aesthetics and design – function). There is no
absolutely right or wrong approach; it all depends on what the
information is to be used for. The result of this type of coding can

be presented as a table such as Table 9.6. In this case the table shows
the responses from 70 respondents (ie those not intending to buy).
Note that the columns do not total 100 per cent; this is because of
multi-response – some respondents gave a reason for not intending
to buy that falls in two or more code categories. Tables showing this
type of coded response to open-ended questions can of course also
include cross analyses.

Table 9.6 *Reasons for not considering buying the appliance*
(those not considering)

Reason	%
Design of appliance	35
Cost factors	25
Unreliability of appliance	21
Have no need for appliance	18
Don't know	10
Total	*
Base	70

* Multi-response and therefore the column does not total 100.

A final type of analysis to mention is of questions which produce
responses in the form of numerical values, eg:

Q11 How much did you pay for this appliance?
     DO NOT PROMPT. RECORD ACTUAL VALUE.
     £ ...

The individual responses can be listed, sorted into order (eg by
descending value) and then classified into intervals as illustrated
in Table 9.7. It will be seen that the intervals are not of equal
range and this is deliberate since most responses fell into the
narrow range of £340–345. The question responses could have
been recorded under pre-coded intervals but without knowing
the likely responses, it is very possible that the wrong intervals
could have been used, eg £340–350 would have accounted for
two-thirds of all responses, and there would have been no indication of whether most would tend to the top or bottom end of
this range.

Table 9.7 *Amount paid for appliance (those who have bought the appliance in the last two years)*

Amount paid £	%
Under 300	3
301–340	19
340–345	54
345–350	13
350	7
Don't know/can't remember	4
Total	**100**
Base	58

As well as showing the distribution of numerical values by intervals (as in Table 9.7) various statistical measures could be used to describe the responses, such as median and modal values, range and inter-quartile ranges. Such measures are often particularly useful and may be used in grossing up from the sample to the total population (eg having calculated the average consumption of a product among the sample, the level amongst the whole population might be estimated by multiplying this average by the known total population).

METHODS OF QUANTITATIVE DATA ANALYSIS

So far we have just shown the output sought from data analysis. How in practice is the work done? The simplest method, if the most laborious, is 'hand' analysis. This requires no more resources than pen and paper and some patience. At its simplest, hand analysis involves counting the responses by going through the questionnaires and marking the responses on a check sheet; 'five-bar gating' is commonly used, eg:

Q8   Ownership of the appliance
   Yes   ̶ ̶ ̶ ̶ ̶ ̶ ̶ ̶
         Total = 40
   No   ̶ ̶ ̶ ̶ ̶ ̶ ̶ ̶ ̶ ̶ ̶ ̶
         Total = 60

Alternatively the questionnaires can be sorted into piles with common responses to a question (eg 'yes' and 'no' piles) and each pile then counted. With this method cross analysis is possible, for example to produce a tenure split as per Table 9.3. The questionnaires would be first sorted into two piles – owner occupiers and tenants – and then each of these piles further sorted between appliance owners and non-owners. With time and patience any cross analysis can be produced in this way.

Another method of hand analysis is to transfer the responses (or key ones) onto a data sheet. An example is shown below with each respondent allocated a line and each question/response a column.

Respondent	Question				
	Q1 Type of metal			Q2 Consumption	Q3 Source
	Steel	Copper	Other	£ 000	In-house	Out
1	*	*		5	*	
2		*		13		*
3	*			2	*	
etc						

Figure 9.1 *Example of a data-logging sheet*

Data sheets of this sort are often a good way of analysing industrial and business research questionnaires. Columns can be totalled and averaged and if necessary easily adjusted for errors or new estimates. Also simple relationships between responses can be searched for (eg do those with an in-house supply have a higher level of consumption than those buying out?).

Whilst it is important to understand the principles of hand analysis, few will want to use it except perhaps for very small samples. Nearly everyone has access to a PC and computer analysis is quicker, less laborious, more accurate and in practice capable of producing far more sophisticated output. The basic software choice is between adapting general purpose software or using specialised survey analysis packages.

General software that is likely to be already installed in application suites such as MS Office or Perfect Office and which can be used for data analysis and includes spreadsheets such as Excel and databases such as Approach. A spreadsheet is much like the hand data-logging sheet just discussed, but once set up offers advantages in terms of ease of input (and legibility of what is entered), automatic calculation and re-calculation and facilities to sort data. Like data-logging sheets, the spreadsheet rows are used for each respondent and columns for questions. Databases allow questionnaires to be entered individually and then aggregated to produce tables including cross analysis and statistical calculations.

Such general purpose software has the advantage of low cost (usually it is already installed) and is likely to be the option for a 'do your own' researcher with a limited and infrequent requirement. However, setting up spreadsheets or designing a database takes time and some skill, and needs to be tested and de-bugged. Also the sophistication of the output is likely to be limited. If there is a regular data analysis requirement, it may, therefore, be better to consider one of the packages that have been specially developed for market research. These vary in cost (from a few hundred pounds upwards), sophistication and ease of use (from the very simple to those requiring training courses to become adept). Suppliers of such packages can be found in the market research press (particularly the monthly *Research* published by the Market Research Society). Another alternative is to buy-in data analysis as a service, and for a 'do your own' researcher with an occasional need this may be a better approach than buying and learning how to use software. Buying such a service will be mentioned again in the next chapter.

If either specialised software or a bought-in service is used, the data analysis process is normally carried out in several distinct stages. Firstly, open ended questions are coded as discussed earlier – a coding frame is developed from all responses or a sample of them and the responses to these questions in each questionnaire are then given a code (it is written in). Next the codes and the responses from pre-coded questions are inputted; the specific method of such data entry will depend on the package (although nearly all data entry is based on numeric codes). A simple analysis called a 'hole count' is then often produced to give top-line results and provide a quality check. The final tables can then be specified (eg question number, labelling, filtering, cross breaks, inclusion of mean scores, etc) and then run to produce the desired output. If data analysis is bought-in, the supplier may take over all this process, although they will require some guidance on the final output required.

QUALITATIVE DATA ANALYSIS

In qualitative research the samples are usually smaller than those in quantitative surveys. However, the data may (or should) be more subtle and complex. It is likely for example that questions will be mainly open ended and the interviewer will have prompted for full responses. Also the interview or discussion may be unstructured with the sequence and even range of topics covered varying between different respondents. Some of the methods of data analysis already discussed for quantitative research, including data-logging sheets, are applicable to qualitative research as well. However, coding open-ended responses is seldom appropriate since too much detail is lost in this way and it is more usual to list and compare full responses. If the number of responses is few enough it may be enough just to read through the relevant parts of the questionnaires or other records. It is also often useful to make photocopies of each questionnaire and then cut them up and sort them into common topics (each cut piece should have a respondent identifier). Often in the report produced of the research it will be appropriate to illustrate with verbatim quotations from individual respondents, and sorting in this way will make this easier. Responses can also be transcribed on a word processing or database package and this will facilitate electronic rather than manual sorting, but the benefits of this have to weighed against the work involved.

Where interviews or group discussions have been tape recorded – a common practice in qualitative research – it is generally considered good practice to transcribe them into typed-up text and carry out analysis with this material. However, it may be enough to simply listen to the tapes and take notes, and arguably even if full transcription is carried out the tapes should still be used as well, to capture some nuances lost in the text. It will be obvious that whilst tape recording is efficient at the interview it imposes much additional work afterwards and this is one reason why qualitative research is expensive either to do or to buy-in.

A final comment on data analysis is that the notes from desk research may need sorting and integrating into a coherent whole. This may have been done before any fieldwork element to the project was even planned. In this work it is important to preserve the source of desk research data so that its reliability can be considered when the report is put together or presented.

REPORTING

Having analysed the fieldwork data and integrated desk research notes, the results of the research project need reporting. If the researcher and research user are one and the same a formal report will not be necessary, although even in this case the data need sorting and arranging in some way so that the results and their implications are clear and there is a record for future reference. However, it is unusual for research results to be just of interest to the researcher and it is far more common for the researcher to communicate the results to others – colleagues, superiors, outside advisors, providers of finance, etc. In the case of professional research the communication is with a client. The reporting stage is, therefore, concerned with effective communication of the results to those who are going to take some action on the basis of what they learn from the research results. Often this audience will lack any market research knowledge and clarity is essential. To do the research work justice and increase the chances that it is used effectively, thought (and time), therefore, need to be given to preparing an effective report.

There are two basic forms of reporting: written reports and personal presentations. A competent researcher should know how to put together a good written report and most of this section is concerned with this sort of communication. However, often research is more effectively communicated face to face: 'clients' often lack the time or inclination to read through lengthy reports. Quite often, however, both types of reporting are appropriate with a written report following a presentation, although possibly the material may be little more than copies of the visual aids used in the meeting.

Whether a report is written or in the form of a presentation it needs structure. At primary school you were perhaps taught that every story needs a beginning, a middle and an end. This is not a bad rule for market research reports. The beginning is an introduction, the middle is the findings of the research and the end is the conclusions.

An *introduction* meets the reader's or audience's need to know why the research was carried out (background), what information was sought (objectives) and how it was obtained (research methods). With this out of the way, the findings can be understood in context.

The background element of the introduction need only be brief; a paragraph or even a sentence is usually sufficient, eg:

> The Magnificent Marble Company is considering marketing a revolutionary style of slab and Truefacts were commissioned to carry out research on the potential acceptability of the new product.

The second part of the introduction should be the research objective and a listing of the main information areas covered to meet this objective. As argued in Chapter 2, every project should have formal, explicit objectives and a defined information coverage, written down in some form at the start of the research. At the reporting stage, therefore, there should be no difficulty stating what these were.

The final part of the introduction is a description of the methods used in the research. If fieldwork has been used this might be a substantial section with details of sampling, interviewing techniques and fieldwork timing provided. A copy of any questionnaires used should be attached to the report (eg in the appendix – see shortly). In a purely desk research study the methods section can be much briefer, eg:

> The information for this report was collected through desk research from published sources and by database searching. A list of the key sources is appended (Appendix 1).

The research *findings* part of a report is very much the meat of the document; it is a presentation of the relevant data that has come out of the research. Relevant, though, is an important qualification. The data presented should meet the objectives of the research and not be thrown in just because you have come across it or even because it may be vaguely interesting. Findings are the facts meeting the objectives; no more and no less.

Findings should also be principally statements of facts, rather than the report author's opinions. There is a place for the researcher to give an opinion, but it is not here. The facts may, of course, be others' opinions, where they are themselves significant in the market – eg opinions of buyers to the service provided by suppliers. However, the researcher should in such cases make sure that it is transparent whose opinions are being referred to (ie the market's and not the researcher's own opinions). This can avoid some serious misunderstandings, particularly if negative views on a company's products or service standards are being reported.

Findings are, therefore, statements of what is or what might be and not what ought to be. However, it is sometimes useful to provide some 'pointers' leading to the later conclusions. In the example below the 'pointer' is in bold text.

> The market has shrunk by an average of 5% per annum through-out the latter 1980s and early 1990s. **This fact may be relevant to the market entry decision.**

The findings section of the report (whether written or verbal) should be organised in some logical sequence of subjects. In a report of the structure of a market, for example, the order of the main headings might be:

1. Product analysis
2. Market size by sector
3. Past and recent trends
4. Suppliers and their market shares
5. Distribution
6. Marketing methods
7. Market forecasts

A report may include findings from both desk research and field-work. Bearing in mind that the audience for the report will generally be more interested in what has been found than how it was found, it is better to integrate the findings by theme rather than have separate desk research and fieldwork sections. If, for example, desk research data include market share estimates and fieldwork includes consumers' satisfaction with suppliers, the two subjects could come together in the 'suppliers' section of the report. It should be clear, however, which data are from the fieldwork and which from desk sources. Desk research sources should also be explicitly referenced; the reader then knows the 'authority' of the data, whilst a researcher can trace sources in any follow-on research.

The purpose of the *conclusions* section of a report is often mis-understood, even by researchers claiming some experience. Conclusions are not a summary, although some of the main findings may well be repeated. Nor are conclusions the same as recommendations; these go one step further and follow conclusions. Conclusions should tell the reader or audience the 'so what' of the research – significant implications of the findings. They are of course rooted in the facts, but go beyond and necessarily include opinion; the researcher's opinion. For example:

The sector of the owner occupier market without central heating is predominantly found in the lower income groups (65 per cent in the D and E social class groups). This should be taken into account in developing new product packages and particularly in relation to pricing and finance deals.

In the example, the first sentence reiterates findings mentioned earlier in the report (with a proportion quoted in brackets to give authority to the statement). The second sentence, however, goes further and considers the implications and includes the report author's opinion. To prepare effective conclusions the researcher needs an understanding of the interests and wider commercial objectives of the decision-makers who are the report's audience (eg to increase sales of central heating appliances and particularly to first-time homes).

Beyond conclusions are recommendations, eg:

The Company should develop a simple central heating package to be installed at costs of under £700 and backed by low repayment finance deals.

In this case the report is not just stating the implications of the research, but is now saying specifically what should be done. If the recommendations are accepted, the company will be committed to action, expenditure and risk.

The introduction, findings and conclusions are the main elements in a market research report, whether it is verbal and face-to-face or a written document. Two other parts of a report are a summary and appendices. A *summary* is required in a written report of any length (eg if the findings are more than five pages). It should be short – no more than 5 per cent of the length of the findings. Often summaries are hastily written at the last minute. This is a mistake. The summary will often be more carefully read than the full report. Writing the summary is also a good test of the findings section – if you find it difficult to summarise large parts of the findings, it is probably because they do not say anything. It is not true that some findings are so complex (qualitative researchers say 'rich') that they cannot be summarised; they are almost certainly just waffle.

It is generally agreed that in written reports a summary is best bound at or near the front of the report, precisely where is a matter of opinion. Some favour having the summary as the very first section, in which case it should summarise the introduction and the conclusions as well as the findings. Others prefer a summary after the introduction and some recommend that the conclusions should follow (and precede the main findings). These are matters of personal preference.

Verbal presentations often do not include a summary. Where the range of data is quite small this is appropriate, but if the research findings are complex and lengthy, there is a strong argument for summarising after discussing the findings in detail and before the conclusions are presented.

Appendices in written reports include material to which the reader may wish to refer but probably not initially. For example, an appendix is a suitable place to list the sources consulted in desk research, and in fieldwork research, and the questionnaires are usually attached as an appendix. Other possibilities include samples of product literature and possibly photocopies of particularly useful articles or tables of detailed statistics. However, resist the temptation to include everything, even of the remotest interest, found in the research. Such material can be kept on file rather than used to fill out the report to an unmanageable size.

The tools of a written report are words, tables and charts of various sorts. The best advice about words is to keep them simple; avoid jargon and technical terms (unless you are really confident that they are understood). Reports are not works of literature and it is best to keep blocks of text short – a few simple sentences (but don't make every sentence a separate paragraph). Make liberal use of headings and sub-headings or consider using 'headlines' instead, eg:

Tenants have not taken up central heating

Statistical data should be presented in the form of tables, for example as illustrated earlier in this chapter, or charts, rather than set out in text form. Any such tables should be self descriptive with adequate titles and labelling. The text accompanying tables should refer to them (preferably above rather than after the table) but should not just describe in words what the table shows. Rather the significant point of the table should be highlighted, eg:

> Owner occupiers appear to be more likely to consider purchasing the appliance than tenants; 58% of owner occupiers are 'very' or 'fairly' likely to purchase compared to 23% amongst tenants.

Tables certainly have a place, but many non-researchers find them difficult to read and it is often better to show statistical data in chart form: histograms, bar charts, pies or trend lines (historical series of data are always better communicated in such a form). At one time this involved laborious work and some draughtsmanship. However, electronics have again made things much easier and most PC owners will have a suitable graphics package. Charts and graphics can also be used to communicate concepts.

When it comes to the format of a written report, a hand-written report on scrap paper, arguably, does all that is required. It is unlikely, however, to impress or enhance the reputation of the author. With computers, high quality printers and word processing software available in nearly all offices, there is really no excuse for a poor standard of written report presentation. Professional quality documents can now be put together with only the minimum of skill.

As already mentioned, face-to-face presentations are often a more effective way of communicating the research results than in a written report. The key tool here is of course the human voice. The late A J P Taylor could speak for half an hour on television without any apparent notes and no visual aids and make the re-unification of Italy into a fascinating story. However, few of us have such skills, and even he might have struggled if the 'story' material was largely statistical. Charts and other visual material are, therefore, essential and need to be prepared with as much care as a written report. The format depends on resources and the size of the audience, and can include A4 sheets for one-to-one presenta-tions, flipcharts and overhead projection slides (easily prepared on computers and copiers). Computer packages such as Powerpoint also facilitate presentations given completely on-screen. In a one-to-one meeting a normal PC screen is adequate to show such a presentation but for larger audiences a larger monitor or a computer linked projector will be required; these can be hired as required. Whatever format is used, charts should be simple; summary tables only, graphs without too much detail and words in bullet points rather than long text.

During the actual presentation it is bad practice to read through everything on each presentation chart; assume the audience can read and they should certainly be able to make out any wording put on the screen. Instead fill in the details of the charts and talk round them. The degree to which the presentation is scripted may depend on the audience, the importance of the event and the your own skill. Most people need to script and rehearse to do their best and also to make sure they do not overrun (or underrun) the time slot allocated.

10

Buying Market Research

Although this is a book about doing market research, there are limits to what can be achieved on a 'do your own' basis. Some research requirements will be clearly beyond any in-house resources and skills. In this situation the alternative is to buy-in. This may involve handing the whole project over to a professional agency (commissioning full service research) but this is not the only option; buying published research or using outside suppliers for part of the project can also be considered. This chapter outlines each option but starts with a description of the organisations that offer various types of market research services.

SUPPLIERS – THE MARKET RESEARCH INDUSTRY

The supply of market research is a significant if not massive UK industry. In 1997 at least £800 million was spent on professionally provided research services and this does not include the value of all published research data. The range of subjects and forms in which these services are delivered is enormous. Research is carried out in virtually all markets and for all kinds of businesses, although food and drink account for the largest slice of the total research spend. Market research services are also bought by non-commercial organisations – in its various guises the Government is the largest buyer. Forms in which research is delivered include *ad hoc* full service research commissioned by individual clients, syndicated and continuous research to which buyers subscribe, and published research in various forms. Research can also be bought as partial services, such as fieldwork only.

There are about 300 UK suppliers – market research agencies – whose main business is market research and allied activities (eg opinion polling) supplying these services. There are also other organisations who carry out this sort of work alongside their mainstream activities (eg management consultancies). The specialists range in size from operations with turnovers approaching £100 million (Taylor Nelson AGB, the largest, had billings of around £80 million in 1997), through medium-sized companies with turnovers of a couple of millions upwards, to very many small agencies and one man bands – of the 400 specialist suppliers, less than 50 have a turnover exceeding £1 million. The larger suppliers offer a wide range of services and specialisms, although the top ten agencies derive the majority of their income from syndicated and continuous rather than *ad hoc* research. Smaller agencies are more likely to specialise either in markets (eg food, business to business, etc) or in a particular type of research – many of the smaller ones are exclusively in qualitative research. Most agencies offer a high level of expertise in at least a few areas and nearly all are at least competent in something. Unlike some other businesses, there are few rogues and charlatans in market research.

The trade association of UK market research companies is the British Market Research Association (BMRA)* formed in 1998 as a result of a merger of two separate bodies (AMSO and ABMRC). Membership of this organisation implies a commitment to professionalism and quality – member companies are expected to be assessed to the recognised quality standards of the Market Research Quality Standards Association (MRQSA) by 2001. These standards define minimum levels for managing and conducting market research and incorporate the earlier fieldwork standards of the Interviewer Quality Control Scheme (IQCS). Confusingly, IQCS will also continue independently for the immediate future and provide some assurance that at least an agency's data collection meets recognised minimum standards.

The staffing of market research agencies is at two levels: professional and support staff. The staff who design research, plan it, write reports and meet clients are generally educated to at least first degree level and have additional vocational training – in this sense market research is a profession, if not a regulated one (as is, say, law). Nearly all such practitioners are members of a professional body – the Market Research Society (MRS) – whose activities include education and training, promoting the worth and standing of

---

*   Contact details for organisations, companies and publications mentioned in this chapter are provided at the end of the chapter.

research, and operating a code of practice to protect the interests of research suppliers, buyers and respondents. Membership of the MRS is, however, individual; agencies as such cannot be members and the Society can only regulate suppliers indirectly.

Most people working in market research, however, are not professional level staff; they are interviewers and other support workers. Interviewers are the most well known face of market research through their contact with the general public – door to door, on streets and by phone. Interviewers are very largely female, mainly work part time or casually, often for several agencies and usually remotely from agency head office or direct supervision. The quality of the research, however, depends very largely on their work and it is for this reason that IQCS was set up. This scheme, now also incorporated in MRQSA, sets minimum standards for initial training and continuous monitoring of work, and includes an assessment system to ensure member companies' compliance.

From this brief description it should be apparent that the market research industry is structured and organised if rather fragmented and is in part a 'cottage' business. It, however, provides a more than adequate choice of suppliers to meet virtually any market research needs. The difficulty faced by a novice buyer is finding the right agency to meet his or her particular need. Some of the sources available from which to locate potential suppliers include the membership directories of the trade association (BMRA) and, possibly the most comprehensive, the *MRS Organisation Book*.

We will now discuss the various ways in which market research can be bought.

BUYING PUBLISHED RESEARCH

Over 30,000 published research reports are available and cover virtually all markets and businesses. These range in price from the very modest (less than £100) to the quite expensive (over £10,000). What they all have in common is that they are produced speculatively by their publishers rather than to meet the needs of a specific client and it is for this reason that they cost very much less than equivalent specially commissioned research. This is particularly so for international research – many published reports have an international scope (as well as those covering individual non-UK markets). Locating relevant published research and considering whether it meets some or all the research requirements should, therefore, be a first step in buying research.

It should also be considered before undertaking any significant 'do your own' fieldwork, and is arguably part of the desk research discussed in Chapter 3.

Publishers of market research reports include several who specialise in this business and who regularly produce linked series of reports. Three such publishers of reports covering consumer markets – UK and international in scope – are: Mintel, the Economist Intelligence Unit (well known for its Retail Business series of reports) and Euromonitor. A specialist in technical and industrial markets is Frost & Sullivan. Apart from these and other regular publishers covering a wide range of markets, there are very many organisations producing reports on specialised subjects or on an occasional basis. Sources for locating such titles include *Market Search*, and *Findex* (good for US and international reports). Reports can also be located on-line and some of them can also be accessed in this way (though they still have to be paid for).

Publishers of at least significantly priced reports produce freely available brochures describing the contents and how the data has been collected and these can be examined before a commitment to purchase is made. For the most expensive it may be possible to look through the report at the publisher's offices. The methods used to prepare the reports should be considered; appropriate methods are identical to those used in *ad hoc* research and just because the reports are printed is no guarantee that the data are reliable (eg based on adequate sized samples). In selecting published research judgement is needed.

For completeness, mention should also be made of syndicated and continuous research data services. These are available at high cost, on subscription and mainly cover retail and food markets. They are generally based on extensive interview programmes or large panels or retail audits. There are relatively few suppliers; mainly the largest companies in the research industry. Such research accounts for a substantial proportion of the total research spend and is an important part of the whole industry. However, these sources are unlikely to be appropriate or affordable by the occasional research buyer. In fact, if you are a serious potential customer for the data you are likely to know the sources already and be regularly contacted by the main suppliers.

COMMISSIONING *AD HOC* FULL SERVICE RESEARCH

A specific and individual research need can be met by a tailored service from a research agency which takes on the whole project from an initial briefing through to presenting the end results. This is *ad hoc,* full service research. Reasons for considering this approach instead of 'do your own' research include a lack of internal resources and skills and sometimes the need for the final research report to carry the authority of an independent professional agency.

Commissioning this sort of research starts with a brief; telling the agency what you require from the research. This should outline why the research is required and how the results will be used (the decisions to be guided). An objective should also be set for the research prior to meeting the agency or in discussion with their staff – see also our discussion in Chapter 2. This briefing may include some indication of the methods it is anticipated the agency might use, although this can be left to them to recommend; they are or should be the experts in this respect. The briefing also needs to include some indication of the budget available for the research; without this information it is difficult for an agency to match a research plan to your needs and resources. It is also essential that a budget is allocated before serious involvement with an agency. Initial discussions may indicate the realistic ballpark and it is unreasonable to put an agency to the trouble of preparing a proposal (invariably at no charge despite the design work involved) if you do not have the money available.

At this point the novice buyer will reasonably want to know how much commissioned research is likely to cost but unfortunately we cannot give any really useful guidance. It all depends on the information sought, the scope of the research (eg whether international) and the methods that are appropriate. All we can say is that research is a skilled and professional service and is priced accordingly, with entry level costs of several thousand pounds and five figures quite normal.

The brief to an agency can be in the form of a written document (and this is useful to help focus the requirement) or informally at a meeting (which will normally be appropriate even if you prepare a written brief). If you are new to buying research or the project is large or unusual it will be sensible to aproach two or three agencies and invite each to prepare proposals. Do no more than this though; it will involve you in too much work and an agency should not be expected to prepare proposals if the chance of commission is less than say one in three. The difficulty, however, is drawing up the shortlist of agencies to invite to quote. Sources such as the *MRS Organisation Book* and the BMRA listings provide lots to choose from, but how does one make an initial selection? Relevant criteria include:

- *Sector experience.* Other things being equal, it is better to use an agency with experience of the market of interest to you; they are more likely to know how to research it. Also they will have a better understanding of the marketing issues involved.
- *Research skills.* If it is obvious that a qualitative approach is needed (or mystery shopping or a quantitative study) select an agency with these skills. However, as a novice buyer you may not know what is appropriate. Also, something to consider in this respect is that the different agencies may suggest quite different approaches to the same brief; in part this is a matter of offering what they are good at, but it also reflects that there is often more than one way to approach the brief.
- *Geography.* Where the agency is based is not usually a major concern but if the research is international in scope their abilities and resources to carry out the work in the countries of interest is an issue.
- *Agency size.* Both large and small agencies can do excellent work but the project should be appropriate to their scale and resources.

The qualifications of agencies in these respects can be initially identified in the published sources and then followed up by phone contact.

Once briefed, the agency or agencies will produce a proposal for the research. This is more than just a quotation and is likely to be a document of up to a dozen pages in length. It should indicate an understanding of why the research is required, state the agreed objective and outline the information to be provided, describe in some detail the methods that will be used, including sample size and selection, interview method and duration, and specify the form of output intended (eg full written report, presentation and charts, etc). A price will also be quoted and this is normally inclusive and fixed within the context of the parameters set out in the rest of the proposal. (If a ten minute interview is envisaged but you subsequently want to extend the coverage to a twenty minute interview, expect to be charged more.) The payment terms requested by agencies normally include a substantial up-front deposit, 40 or 50 per cent. A timetable will also be provided that will normally meet your stated requirements unless these are unrealistic; agencies can be pressurised to meet 'impossible' deadlines but this may diminish the quality of the work and be self-defeating.

Once proposals are received they need evaluating and where two or three are received, compared. The research must firstly meet your requirements and it is important to be sure of these before giving a go-ahead. Possibly not all the requirements can be met because your budget is too tight and this trade-off needs considering carefully. The research methods should at least seem convincing with the reasons for the choices explained. The agency is also likely to indicate their relevant experience and this should be considered in the decision and possibly also followed up in further discussions with agency staff. Lastly there is the question of price and apparent value for money. If you indicate a budget (we recommend you do) alternative proposals are likely to be similarly priced but may well vary in what is offered (eg number of interviews). However, be sceptical of an agency offering vastly more (or charging very much less) than others; possibly there is a gap between your expectations and their intentions. Also, before using an agency for the first time, visit their offices; it is surprising how often big money is spent without this very basic check being made.

Once selected, regard the agency as temporary colleagues, and work with and not against them. The degree of contact during the project may depend on the complexity of the project and your own inclinations. If required, agencies are usually happy to keep at arms length until the project is complete. However, it is common to at least invite clients to approve questionnaires – you may not be able to judge the technical aspects of their design but should be able to at least check that the subjects of interest are covered. Working with an agency is also a learning opportunity for future 'do your own' research, and listening-in to phone interviews, going out with field interviewers, attending groups and seeing data processing work are all likely to be instructive and are usually offered (with varying degrees of enthusiasm) by agencies.

The final output from the agency will be a report or presentation and this should be reviewed critically but without hostility. Have the objectives and coverage been met? Have the methods matched the plan? Are the results well presented and can they be validated against other, independent data? Such evaluations (which should be written up) will be valuable in any future commissioning or if requesting any glaring deficiencies in the work to be put right.

BUYING PARTIAL SERVICES

An alternative to commissioning full service research is to use suppliers to carry out just part of the research process, leaving the rest to be done on a 'do your own' basis. This will offer considerable savings compared to having an agency taking responsibility for all aspects of the work. Interviewing and data processing are the most common parts to put out, especially in consumer research. Despite all we have written in earlier chapters, carrying out face-to-face or even phone interviews with samples of 200 or more consumers is just not practicable for one person, and processing the completed questionnaires is also a daunting task. However, having decided on appropriate methods, including type of interviewing and sampling details, and designed the questionnaire, the actual interviewing work and processing of the completed questionnaires can be passed across to an agency as a 'field and tab' commission.* Recruitment of respondents to attend group discussions or depth interviews can also be bought-in as a separate service. The output back is normally tables giving a full analysis (to your specification) of the completed questionnaires. These can then be used to prepare an 'in-house' report or presentation.

Most market research agencies offering full service research will also work on a 'field and tab' basis. However, there are also a number of agencies that specialise in this sort of service (ie they do not offer full service research). The *MRS Organisation Book* is one of the best sources to identify potential suppliers. In 'field and tab' commissions, the agency's sector experience is probably less important; what counts is their skill in the type of fieldwork envisaged. The process of selection is broadly the same as for full service but the proposal is likely to be little more than a quotation – with 'field and tab' it is not up to the agency to select an appropriate research

---

*   Just interviewing without processing can also be bought – field only – although in most cases there would be little point to this. Similarly data processing can be bought separately from one of half a dozen or so companies specialising in this work (they mainly work for agencies without their own in-house data processing resources).

design or decide on the information coverage. These are the client's responsibilities. Similarly, the specification to suppliers needs to be more specific in terms of method and the agency will be less accommodating if these are changed by the client once the work starts (the agency's margins are rather less for 'field and tab'). Also the client is expected to design the basic questionnaire – although the agency may tidy it up and format it – and take responsibility for any deficiencies in its design. The lower cost of 'field and tab' reflects the reduced responsibilities of the agency compared to full service research.

Omnibus surveys

A variant on 'field and tab' services is buying into omnibus surveys. The cost of carrying out an interview increases with its length, but not pro rata; whether the interview is face-to-face or by phone, there are significant set-up costs regardless of how long it takes – respondents must be located and persuaded to cooperate, there is travel time for face-to-face interviews and wasted calls if the interview is conducted by phone, and there are also administrative tasks connected with each interview. Other things being equal, therefore, the marginal costs of adding questions to an interview tend to fall and this is the economic basis of omnibus surveys. Some agencies regularly (eg weekly, monthly) interview specified samples face-to-face or by phone, eg housewives, men, motorists or senior business decision-makers. The numbers involved are often substantial; 1000 or more interviews in each wave. The subjects of the interview consist of questions put on the omnibus by a number of subscribers; in other words space is sold in question slots. Just one or many questions can be bought at a time, although the need to accommodate several subscribers puts some limits on what can be included from one client. Also, beyond some number of questions it would be as cheap to have an *ad hoc* sample. As with other sorts of 'field and tab' research, the output from omnibus surveys is a tabulation – of each subscriber's questions cross analysed by the standard demographic question included in the interviews.

Omnibuses, therefore, offer the opportunity to collect data from large and often rigorous samples at relatively low cost and far less than would be involved in a comparable *ad hoc* sample. Omnibuses can meet a range of applications including those listed below.

Toe in the water research

Omnibus research is often used to obtain basic information about a market and possibly to supplement desk research. This may be done prior to planning a full *ad hoc* research programme. Similarly, omnibuses can be used where the *ad hoc* information need is limited in range.

Supplementary research

Sometimes, however well planned, *ad hoc* research leaves some critical questions unanswered or requires additional detail to be obtained before a marketing decision is taken. One or two questions on an omnibus survey can answer this need and, with the quick turnrounds offered, will meet most decision deadlines.

Minority samples

We are not sure what proportion of the population buys a pair of walking boots in a year but it will be in single figure percentages. The only way to locate such a group of consumers may be to contact a sample of, say, all adults until the required sample of buyers is found (assuming that 3 per cent are buyers of boots, to interview only 200 would require initial contacts with 6666) and on an *ad hoc* basis this can be very expensive. Omnibus surveys provide a cost-effective alternative providing the range of information required from the minority sample is limited. The weekly or monthly omnibus may provide sufficient initial contacts, but if not, samples can be aggregated (eg over a month, a weekly 2000 respondent omnibus will cover 8000 – sufficient for our boots example).

Tracking

Omnibus surveys also offer the facility for cost-effective continuous tracking research – monitoring responses over a period. This application can be used in advertising research (eg monitoring brand awareness over a campaign period) and for many other marketing applications.

Are there any disadvantages or problems with omnibus research? Apart from the intrinsic limitations (eg cost effective for only a limited number of questions), the major concern is perhaps quality of response. With omnibus questionnaires covering a very wide range of unrelated topics, the quality of response is arguably less than in a coherent and focused *ad hoc* interview. This is likely to apply particularly to later questions in an omnibus interview (hence clients often push to have their questions placed earlier rather than later). For this reason, some consider omnibus surveys best suited to simple factual type questions rather than those requiring greater respondent concentration and involvement.

It is mainly the larger agencies which offer omnibus surveys. The *MRS Organisation Book*'s service classifications include omnibuses and this source can be used to locate suppliers. However, except for some of the more specialised ones, most omnibus surveys are advertised every month in *MRS Research* (also in *Marketing Week* and *Admap*) and this may be a more convenient way of finding a suitable survey – the adverts include broad details of the samples. The agencies concerned can then be contacted for further details and costings. Omnibus surveys are sold on a rate card basis with a basic charge per closed question with supplements for open-ended questions and other variants. Discounts are available for buying into surveys long term and may be negotiated on other grounds.

Useful contact details

Admap NTC Publications Ltd, Farm Road, Henley on Thames, Oxfordshire R99 1EJ. Tel: 01491 411000.

BMRA 16 Creighton Avenue, London N10 1NO. Tel: 0181 444 3692.

EIU (Economist Intelligence Unit) 15 Regent Street, London SW1Y 4LR. Tel: 0171 930 8763.

Euromonitor 61 Briton Street, London EC1M 5NA. Tel: 0171 251 8024.

Findex Available through Euromonitor (see above).

Frost & Sullivan 4 Grosvenor Gardens, London SW1W 0DH. Tel: 0171 730 3438.

IQCS (Interviewer Quality Control Scheme) **MRQSA** (Market Research Quality Standards Association) 6 Walkfield Drive, Epsom Downs, Surrey KT18 5UF. Tel: 01737 354369.

MRS (Market Research Society) 15 Northburgh Street, London EC1V 0AH. Tel 0171 490 4911.

Market Search 1 Hay Hill, Berkley Square, London W1X 7LF. Tel: 0171 495 1940.

Marketing Week St Giles House, Poland Street, London W1V 4AX. Tel: 0171 439 4222.

Mintel 18 Long Lane, London EC1A 9HE. Tel: 0171 606 4533.

Bibliography

GENERAL READING ON MARKET RESEARCH (CONSUMER RESEARCH ORIENTATED)

Aaker, David A & George S Day (1990) *Marketing Research*, John Wiley, Chichester.

Baker, Michael J (1991) *Research for Marketing*, Macmillan, London.

Birn, R, Hague, P & Vangelder, P (eds) (1990) *A Handbook of Market Research Techniques*, Kogan Page, London.

Birn, Robin (1991) *The Effective Use of Market Research*, Kogan Page, London.

Cannon, Tom (1973) *Advertising Research*, Intertext, Aylesbury.

Chisnall, Peter (1991) *The Essence of Marketing Research*, Prentice-Hall, Englewood Cliffs, New Jersey.

Chisnall, Peter (1992) *Marketing Research*, McGraw-Hill, Maidenhead.

Crimp, Margaret (1990) *The Marketing Research Process*, Prentice-Hall, Englewood Cliffs, New Jersey.

Crouch, Sunny (1984) *Marketing Research for Managers*, Heinemann, Oxford.

Ehrenberg, ASC (1988) *Repeat Buying*, Edward Arnold, Sevenoaks.

Gordon, Wendy & Roy Langmaid (1988) *Qualitative Market Research*, Gower, Aldershot.

Gorton, Keith & Isobel Doole (1989) *Low-Cost Marketing Research*, John Wiley & Sons, Chichester.

Green, P & Tull, J (1978) *Research for Marketing Decisions*, Prentice-Hall, Englewood Cliffs, New Jersey.

Hague, Paul N & Peter Jackson (1990) *How to Do Marketing Research*, Kogan Page, London.

Jain, AK, Pinson, P & Ratchford, B (1982) *Marketing Research – Applications and Problems*, John Wiley & Sons, Chichester.

Kreuger, Richard A (1989) *Focus Groups (A Practical Guide for Small Business)*, Sage Publications, London.

Robson, S & Foster, A (eds) (1989) *Qualitative Research in Action*, Edward Arnold, Sevenoaks.

Talmage, PA (1988) *Dictionary of Marketing Research*, Market Research Society, London.

Walker, R (ed) (1985) *Applied Qualitative Research*, Gower, Aldershot.

Williams, Keith (1981) *Behavioural Aspects of Marketing*, Heinemann, Oxford.

Worcester, RM & Downam, J (eds) (1986) *Consumer Market Research Handbook*, Elsevier, The Netherlands.

GENERAL READING ON INDUSTRIAL MARKET RESEARCH

Hague, Paul N & Peter Jackson (1992) *Marketing Research in Practice*, Kogan Page, London.

Maclean, Ian (ed) (1976) *Handbook of Industrial Marketing Research*, Kluwer-Harrap, Brentford.

Stacey, NAH & Aubrey Wilson (1963) *Industrial Market Research – Management Techniques*, Hutchinson, London.

Sutherland, Ken (ed) (1991) *Researching Business Markets*, Kogan Page in association with the Industrial Marketing Research Association, London.

Wilson, Aubrey (1968) *The Assessment of Industrial Markets*, Hutchinson, London.

QUESTIONNAIRES

Hague, Paul (1993) *Questionnaire Design*, Kogan Page, London.

Oppenheim, AN (1970) *Questionnaire Design and Attitude Measurement*, Heinemann, Oxford.

Wolfe, A (1984) *Standardised Questions*, Market Research Society, London.

PRESENTATIONS AND REPORT WRITING

Hague, Paul and Roberts, Kate (1994) *Presentations and Report Writing*, Kogan Page, London.

Jay, Anthony (1976) *Slide Rules*, Video Arts, London.

May, John (1982) *How to make Effective Business Presentations*, McGraw-Hill, London.

DESK RESEARCH

Jackson, Peter (1994) *Desk Research*, Kogan Page, London.

STATISTICS

Hague, Paul and Harris, Paul (1993) *Sampling and Statistics*, Kogan Page, London.

BUYING MARKET RESEARCH

Jackson, Peter (1994) *Buying Market Research*, Kogan Page, London.

Jackson, Peter (1997) *Quality in Market Research*, Kogan Page, London.

JOURNALS AND PERIODICALS

Business Marketing Digest (formerly *Industrial Marketing Digest*), quarterly, Wallington, Surrey.

Harvard Business Review, bi-monthly, Boston, Mass, USA.

Journal of the Market Research Society, quarterly, London.

Marketing, weekly, London.

Index

University of South Wales
Treforest Library
Tel: 01443 483400